CAREERING

(v): Taking action to become the most powerful,
valuable, fulfilled version of yourself.

GOTHAM BOOKS

Published by Penguin Group (USA) Inc.
375 Hudson Street, New York, New York 10014, U.S.A.

Penguin Group (Canada), 10 Alcorn Avenue, Toronto, Ontario, Canada
M4V 3B2 (a division of Pearson Penguin Canada Inc.); Penguin Books
Ltd, 80 Strand, London WC2R 0RL, England; Penguin Ireland, 25 St
Stephen's Green, Dublin 2, Ireland (a division of Penguin Books Ltd);
Penguin Group (Australia), 250 Camberwell Road, Camberwell, Victoria
3124, Australia (a division of Pearson Australia Group Pty Ltd); Penguin
Books India Pvt Ltd, 11 Community Centre, Panchsheel Park, New Delhi
- 110 017, India; Penguin Group (NZ), Cnr Airborne and Rosedale Roads,
Albany, Auckland, New Zealand (a division of Pearson New Zealand Ltd);
Penguin Books (South Africa) (Pty) Ltd, 24 Sturdee Avenue, Rosebank,
Johannesburg 2196, South Africa

PUBLISHED BY GOTHAM BOOKS,
A DIVISION OF PENGUIN GROUP (USA) INC.

RADICAL CAREERING BY SALLY HOGSHEAD
TEXT AND DESIGN COPYRIGHT © 2005 HOGSHEAD MEDIA

GOTHAM BOOKS AND THE SKYSCRAPER LOGO ARE
TRADEMARKS OF PENGUIN GROUP (USA) INC.

RADICAL CAREERING AND THE HOGSHEAD MEDIA LOGO ARE
TRADEMARKS OF SALLY HOGSHEAD. USED BY LICENSE.

First printing: September 2005

ISBN 1-592-40150-3

Printed in the United States of America

VISIT WWW.PENGUIN.COM AND WWW.RADICALCAREERING.COM

Thanks to Headcase Design for conceiving some of the graphic elements.

RADICAL
CAREERING

100 TRUTHS TO JUMPSTART
YOUR JOB, YOUR CAREER,
AND YOUR LIFE

by SALLY HOGSHEAD

design by NUMBER 17, NYC

GOTHAM
BOOKS

To our angel baby

Do you have a career worth loving?

CONTENTS

introduction

THE
10
CHAPTERS OF CAREERING

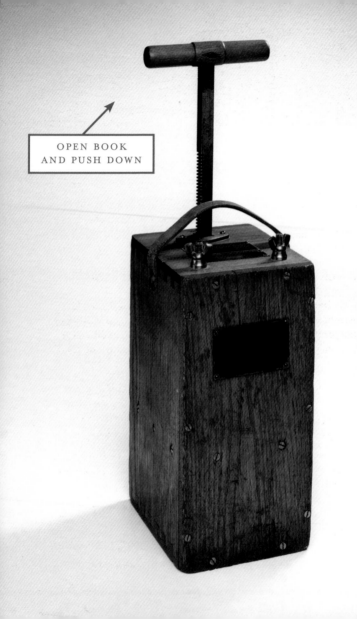

OPEN BOOK
AND PUSH DOWN

Do you have a career worth loving?

Do you cringe at the idea of a mindless job spent shuffling papers and sneaking out at 4:59? Do you want joy and meaning from work? Do you want to kickstart momentum, attack bigger possibilities, and get excited about Monday mornings?

If so, welcome. You're among friends.

To help you create a career worth loving, this book doesn't function like other career books. It doesn't bother with the standard "hang in there, kitty" motivation, or the superficial niceties of your handshake grip. Instead, it's about something infinitely more powerful: building the ultimate version of yourself.

Radical Careering, like careering itself, is visceral. Intuitive. And at times, unreasonable. It's a red-blooded undertaking that you can't intellectualize your way through. Too often we spend hours formatting our resumes, but very little time contemplating what we truly want next in our lives.

The reality is, you already have everything you need to become great. That isn't in any book, only in yourself. This book helps you visualize your no-compromises future, so you can start to build it, piece by piece.

WARNING: This book will automatically self-destruct if left unattended to gather dust on a shelf.

I call those pieces "Radical Truths." Some Truths might reverberate in your mind, giving words to your most personal aspirations and anxieties. Some might become your rallying cry. Some might piss you off. Some might feel brilliant one day and useless the next, depending on your mood. That's fine. If you're the type who dislikes reading books cover-to-cover, use this book like a Magic 8-Ball. Flip to a random page, and see what serendipity has in store for you at that particular moment. Then open the Toolbox and pull out the tool to put that Truth into action.

Maybe you'll find your own personal anthem in here. If that happens, tear it out. Or scrawl it on a stickie note and post it on your computer. Or photo-copy the page and tape it to your mirror. Or whatever else you need to feel inspired on a cold winter's night.

It's not practical to put all the Truths into action at once, so this isn't all or nothing. Go one by one. Piece by piece. Truth by Truth.

While this is a career book, you'll find that many Radical Truths seem unrelated to your career. That's because, for the careerist, life and work feed off each other. Work is personal. Work touches all aspects of our lives. When you're excited about work, it's easier to be excited about all else in your life. And when you're operating as your best self, work is only one of the many areas in which you'll be your best.

One last thing: in modern business, there are no right answers.

Should you wear a suit to the meeting? Who knows. Is it proper to fax a resume? Depends. So the Truths in this book are called "Truths" for a reason. They're not rules. Not gospel. Not absolutes. In fact, there's only one absolute in this whole book: Be the you that you want to be.

You may discover entirely different answers for creating a career worth loving, and I applaud you for finding your own path. When you do, I hope you'll tell me about it, at www.your-radical-path.com.

DON'T JUST READ THIS BOOK.
USE IT.

Excellent question.

BUT FIRST, LET'S CLARIFY WHAT CAREERING ISN'T. CAREERING IS NOT:

WORKING YOURSELF TO DEATH. Chances are, you're already working hard enough. Careering helps you work smarter, faster, and more efficiently, with better focus, bigger goals, and greater appreciation for your own potential.

CLIMBING THE CORPORATE LADDER. Careerists want success, no question. But advancement is a byproduct of a great career, not the goal in and of itself. When you perform at your best, you naturally ascend.

CHASING A BIGGER SALARY. Money may or may not be part of what gives you a career worth loving. Some radical careerists make serious cash, others trade a big salary for a bigger passion. My husband left a high-powered career to stay at home with our kids, because that's his career worth loving.

QUITTING YOUR JOB. Quitting is too easy. Merely trading one business card for another rarely yields true momentum. Instead of just changing jobs, change your role.

RUTHLESS OVERACHIEVING. This isn't pursuing success at any cost. No future is worth compromising your principles for. Ever.

NOW THAT WE'VE GOTTEN THAT OUT OF THE WAY, HERE'S WHAT CAREERING IS.

Careering is the profound, and glorious, and terrifying, and absurdly difficult but infinitely rewarding process of transforming your current self into your ultimate self.

When you're careering, you're being the most powerful, valuable, fulfilled version of yourself. Think back to those times in your career when you performed at your absolute best, when you blew past expectations and quite simply kicked ass. That's when you were careering.

The point of careering goes far beyond money or fame: It bestows the power to do, and have, and be what you love. A radical career allows you to control your future, rather than being controlled by it. It grants true power: The power to become your best self. And even if you don't know what your best self looks like, or feels like, or even does on a day-to-day basis, that's okay. Radical careering is the process of figuring all that out.

Careerists aren't afraid to make big things happen, whether it's on a personal or global level. They ignore the status quo, and build something bigger than themselves. They have the courage to envision the ultimate version of themselves, and the audacity to bring that vision to life. Think Richard Branson and his cheeky Virgin empire, or Steve Jobs and his ultracool iPod. Are they rebels? Or masters of industry? Both. They're radical careerists.

Careerists are crucial within any corporation. They're hardwired for challenge, and expect the same from their co-workers. By boosting their own performance, they often boost revenue and morale. For this reason, careerists are any company's most precious resource.

Careerists become the most valuable people in any company for a very simple reason: They live according to what's possible, instead of being confined by what is.

Of course, that requires breaking a few time-honored rules. As a result, this book isn't for everyone. Slackers won't like it. Drones won't get it. Bureaucrats will burn it.

But let's assume that you're ready to grab the sledgehammer and go at a few conventional formulas. What does your no-compromises future look like? What kind of future could your career help you build? What's stopping you from building it?

That's exactly what we're here to find out.

The birth of the Radical Truths

To do anything great, you have to be a little bit crazy. Well, I did something a lot crazy. I left my own advertising agency, which I'd started at age 27, and opened the L.A. office of the hottest agency in the country. It was a huge professional and financial risk: less money, more pressure. On the upside, it was an ultra-sexy job, awesome challenge, genius company. And opening day was fabulous. Press, parties, congratulations from around the world.

But opening day was September 10, 2001. And you know what day came next.

The following year was nightmarish for everyone. I didn't lose any family or friends. And for that I'm deeply grateful. What I did lose was my sense of self. As the creative director and managing director of a new venture, I was responsible for everyone's jobs. But how do you create momentum from paralysis?

After staking everything, and asking others to do the same, I was crushed by stress and haunted by a sense of failure that I couldn't shake. I slammed into overdrive, working 100-hour weeks to survive during advertising's bleakest year ever.

As the sole breadwinner for my family, the prospect of unemployment was terrifying. However it was the threat of personal failure that tore me apart. Suddenly, for the first time in my life, no matter how I tried, I couldn't produce a successful result. That shocked me.

It truly had never occurred to me that my best wasn't always enough.

My entire career, I'd loved working. Loved it. I'd always set high goals and passionately pursued them. But over the next year, I watched in horror as my career turned on me.

IN CASE OF EMERGENCY ➡ ⬤ ⬅

Nothing I did worked. My confidence plummeted, followed shortly by my performance.

I was preoccupied by questions: How could I reclaim control of my career, instead of feeling controlled by it? Why was I suddenly making decisions based on fear, instead of possibility? When did work stop being fun, and start feeling like…work?

I searched bookstores for help on moving forward. But I couldn't find it. Anywhere. The book I needed didn't exist. Finally, I started looking inside myself. I found my own

"truths." The one thing I did know: Circumstances wouldn't overwhelm me, as long as I focused on the pieces within my control.

Of course, I wasn't the only one who'd been feeling purposeless. Most of us were stuck. Only bankruptcy lawyers were thriving. During this time I received about 50 resumes a week, and since I had no jobs to offer, I ended up mentoring dozens of people. *Creativity* magazine invited me to describe my radical strategies. Within weeks of publishing this "Radical Careering" article, several hundred readers wrote letters to me, and to the magazine, describing how the article affected them.

This response was humbling. It's not like I had all the answers. The truth was, writing the article itself was a feat of radical careering, a way of focusing on the big picture beyond my immediate situation. Mentoring others in their careers helped me find meaning in my own.

Soon after, my husband and I were overjoyed to learn we were expecting twins. Twins! My sense of failure faded away with the blessing of these two little girls. We had something positive to focus on, and that something meant everything.

But our joy didn't last. A few months into the pregnancy, one of the babies died.

Doctors immediately ordered me on bed rest to save the remaining twin. I left everything behind, withdrew to bed, and totally, completely fell apart. This was worse than grief. It was despair.

Lying flat on my back to save one baby, I was forced to contemplate the career that may or may not have caused the loss of the other baby. Was my hard-driving work ethic to

blame? How could I possibly find joy in work ever again? Unemployed and exiled to bed, I was quite literally powerless and alone.

And then, slowly, fate began to appear (in my inbox, of all places). People I'd mentored over the years began contacting me, filling me in on their progress and asking advice. In reality, they now guided me. I began taking my own advice:

Own your career. Live in verbs. Do what you are. Reclaim your life.

I propped my laptop on my growing belly, and I began to write. I wrote for people like me: people who wanted more than success from their careers; they wanted meaning. The more I researched and interviewed and learned about a career worth loving, the more I recovered my sense of purpose. I'd mentored people through my writing before, but this was different. Now I could speak with unconditional compassion and appreciation for the struggle inherent in growth.

As the months passed, the pregnancy progressed well, and so did I. The baby grew big enough to jiggle

my laptop when she kicked.
I wrote the book that I'd so desperately needed to read: a book about reclaiming your career, even amidst brutally difficult circumstances.

This book, which you now hold in your hands, was finished only days before our beautiful daughter Azalea was born.

Looking back, it all happened exactly as it was meant to. As breathtakingly painful as that period was, it forced me to stop and look at my life against a bleak backdrop. My identity was stripped of the fancy job, the salary, the awards. I had to confront who I was—me, as a person—separate from any title or job description. I had to learn about success all over again, from the inside out. I finally got it. Success isn't about being the best. Success is the ongoing process of becoming *your best self.*

Now you know my secret. *Radical Careering* is actually an autobiography.

I didn't blindly stumble upon the ideas in this book, or scavenge them from an MBA program. I earned them. And now I want you to have them.

Whether you're starting your own radical careering journey or already well underway, I have all the respect for you. It can be scary and difficult and painful. But here's the thing:

Scary and difficult and painful don't have to stop you. Scary and difficult and painful are the very things that transform you into your best self.

And for the record: Delivering a baby requires less pain medication than birthing a book.

*Success isn't about
being the best.*

*Success is the process of
becoming your best self.*

THE GLOSSARY OF CAREERING BUZZWORDS

AGE OF INTENSITY: The dawning era in which experiences become our most precious commodity. As life compresses around us, our experiences become increasingly finite, and we search for ways to make the most of every moment.

ALCHEMY: The process of turning a mediocre situation (such as a lame job or relationship) into gold.

CAREER: The sum total of one's entire professional journey, including every job and occupation change along the way. See also: *job.*

CAREERING: Taking action to become the most powerful, valuable, fulfilled version of yourself.

CHRYSALIS: A state of change during which your development isn't obvious to the naked eye, but which will ultimately result in an exquisite transformation.

CLM: "Career Limiting Move." Example: making a pass at your client at the holiday party.

DUPPIES: What CNN named the legions of "Depressed Urban Professionals."

EMAILOPHILE: Someone plugged into email at all times (usually on their CrackBerry).

ENTREPRENEURIAL CLASS: The emerging class of professionals within companies who take responsibility for their performance rather than blindly following bureaucratic norms.

GIG GIGOLO: A job whore. Someone who promiscuously switches employment without consideration for their company or future.

HOTLAP: Scorched spot on your legs caused by a laptop resting on them too long.

INDENTURED SERVITUDE: Feeling trapped in a mediocre job because you lack the skills, network, accolades, or experience to leave in a position of strength. See also: *punching in.*

INSANIA: A jittery, manic high resulting from too much caffeine, adrenaline, and stress.

JOB: Your current employment, including daily tasks, coworkers, title, and workspace. A job is only one component of a career. See also: *career*.

MANTRA STATEMENT: Your life's mission statement. Why you get out of bed in the morning.

MOMENTUM: The rate of speed at which you propel yourself toward goals.

OPTION C: The third option in any form of negotiation. When Option A and Option B aren't acceptable, Option C is the creative course of action you invent to circumvent a barrier.

PERSONAL BRAND: A grown-up version of your reputation. A collection of your attributes: (e.g., skills, knowledge, character) minus liabilities (e.g., unpleasant habit of backstabbing coworkers).

PORTABLE EQUITY: Personal capital that boosts your long-term career opportunity and market value far beyond your current job. Examples: experience, skills, network, industry reputation. See also: *trapped equity*.

PUNCHING IN: Showing up for work without any sense of intention or purpose. Killing time. See also: *indentured servitude*.

TIMESTACKING: Extracting every bit of capacity from time for maximum efficiency. Über multitasking.

TOURIST INDECISION: Anxiety resulting from a sense of being lost or proceeding without clear direction.

TRAPPED EQUITY: Investments of time or effort you can't take with you when you leave a job. Example: your batting average on the company softball team. See also: *indentured servitude*.

VELVET FIST: Brutally hard information or opinions cushioned by a delicate delivery.

VENDOVORE: Person who subsists almost exclusively on Cheetos, Funyons, and other food in the office vending machine.

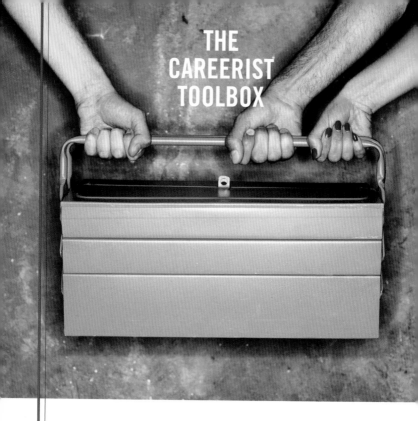

THE CAREERIST TOOLBOX

Inside each chapter, you'll find a "Careerist Toolbox," with tools to help put the Truths into action.

Here's how they work:

INFO TO GO:
Whenever you see this icon, log on to find some seriously cool toys. Each microsite has a different kind of instrument, insight, or inspiration for your own radical careering. For the big enchilada of careering tools, go to www.radicalcareering.com.

THE RADICAL 1000:
How do you compare with other careerists? Check out the results from our groundbreaking survey of more than 1,000 Gen X professionals around the country.

ULTRA CAREERIST ADVICE:
Specific insights on the topic of careering, straight from some of the world's most respected careerists.

INSIDE HOT TIPS:
This is the inside dirt, the privileged tips you can only learn directly from an insider.

THE ICON SAYS:
Quotes from cultural icons and experts of all flavors.

REAL-DEAL ANECDOTES:
These brief stories illustrate a Truth as seen in real-life situations.

AGE OF INTENSITY SIDEBARS:
We're living in the Age of Intensity. Here's how to deal.

RADICAL HOW-TO:
Get radically better results in a specific area, such as conference calls or caffeine boosts.

THE
RADICAL 1000
RESEARCH

Remarkably little up-to-date research exists on the attitudes, priorities, and beliefs of professionals right now. Clearly, tectonic shifts in the corporate arena have led to mass discouragement and uncertainty as the world of business reinvents itself daily. But what about the people who work in this world? What are their deeper issues? What drives them, discourages them, inspires them? What do today's professionals truly want out of their careers?

Less obvious than corporate changes, yet no less dramatic, are the changes in these professionals themselves. Today's rising stars have a different mindset about success. Instead of being motivated by simplistic perks or immediate responsibilities of a JOB, these professionals are driven by an individualistic vision for a lifelong CAREER. They represent a new breed of professionals who adapt to rules that change every morning, and again by lunchtime.

Enter the rise of a new entrepreneurial class*: the careerists.

How, and why, do careerists succeed?

To develop and execute a proprietary study, I enlisted brilliant strategist Linda Jeo Zerba. Linda's research company, Deputy Consulting, deployed researchers to perform in-person interviews in New York, Atlanta, Portland, San Francisco, D.C., Seattle, and Austin; they also conducted phone and email interviews in metropolitan areas such as Chicago, Los Angeles, Houston and Denver. In all, over 1,000 interviews.

To focus our sample, we targeted the 25-to-45 age bracket: Generation X. Hardly a niche, Gen X represents over a third of the workforce, with 65,000,000 workers. Born 1960 to 1980, the youngest are well into their careers, the oldest are approaching middle age. They're post-college, but pre-Boomer.

*ENTREPRENEURIAL CLASS: The emerging class of professionals within companies who take responsibility for their performance, rather than blindly following bureaucratic norms

Conclusions of the Study

CAREERISTS BELIEVE SUCCESS IS A CHOICE.

Throughout the study, without exception, respondents chose the path of personal control over passive acceptance. They work hard not because they "should," as previous generations did, but because they believe their actions make a difference.

Which is the most important in determining success:

Natural talent: 8.8%
Hard work: 91.2%

Which has had the greatest influence on your success:

Luck: 2.3%
Skill set: 15.6%
Reputation: 15.8%
Daily actions: 29.2%
Attitude: 37.1%

Would you rather have a job with:

Security: 15.6%
Opportunity: 84.4%

CAREERISTS VALUE RESPECT OVER CASH.

Refusing to be content with merely a paycheck, careerists value acknowledge-ment, support, and room to do their best work.

Which is more important to get from your employer:

Fat paycheck: 11.2%
Respect: 88.8%

Which is your idea of professional hell:

Long hours: 3.8%
Low pay: 4.7%
Being micromanaged: 15.6%
Disrespectful boss or coworkers: 75.9%

CAREERISTS THINK IN A REVOLUTIONARY WAY.

They actually consume information differently. Raised with Nintendo and MTV, they mentally juggle and multitask with ease, preferring a nonlinear format to rigid patterns. This makes their minds perfectly suited to the Internet, and other forms of unstructured content. (Incidentally, that's why this book functions less like a traditional business tome, and more like a magazine or website.)

Which describes your approach to your career:

Linear thinker (one thing at a time): 27.8%

Lateral thinker (multiple ideas at once): 72.2%

Do you prefer to work:

Within an established structure: 18.7%

In an entrepreneurial environment: 81.3%

Do big changes make you feel:

Stressed about the unknown: 11.4%

Excited about new opportunities: 88.6%

CAREERISTS OPERATE IN A REVOLUTIONARY WAY.

They fiercely value independence, and refuse to allow their employers to define their futures for them. This isn't sullen rebellion; it's a conscious decision to pursue the smartest option rather than blindly follow the majority.

Which best describes your approach to your career:

Wait for results over time: 13%

Create daily momentum: 87%

Which do you prefer:

Being managed: 4.5%

Working autonomously: 95.5%

CAREERISTS POSSESS OPTIMISM AND INTEGRITY.

Unlike the Gordon Gekkonian "greed is good" version of success, careerists seek joy and meaning from work. And while they'll compromise short-term goals for long-term success, they refuse to compromise principles.

Which would you do to boost your long-term chances of success:

Lie about where you went to college: 13.8%

Work every weekend for a year: 26.4%

Take a big pay cut: 29%

Learn a new language: 92.6%

At the peak of your career, what do you realistically expect to earn (assuming 2005 dollars) per year:

Over $300,000: 11.8%

$50,000–$100,000: 15.3%

$100,000–$200,000: 23.1%

$200,000–$300,000: 49.8%

ABOVE ALL, CAREERISTS WANT A CAREER WORTH LOVING.

Which would you choose:
A job I HATE but make three times the money I do now: 13%
A job I LOVE and make half the money I do now: 87%

Power is:
Fame: 2.8%
Making a lot of money: 12%
Access to most important people: 16.3%
Freedom to say no and walk away: 32.3%
Having complete control over your schedule: 36.7%

For careerists, "entrepreneurial" isn't a buzzword. It's a way of life.

Unfortunately, conventional corporations often underutilize their careerists. They tend to interpret entrepreneurialism as disloyalty, independence as defiance, and innovation as lack of focus. However, smart companies realize this talent is their most precious resource. They provide careerists with strategy and parameters, but avoid layered micromanagement. Because careerists seek momentum from both themselves and their companies, employers cannot retrofit them into dusty standardized systems.

The results of this study have expansive implications for anyone interested in hiring, managing, or retaining high-performing talent.

INFO TO GO

What are the implications of The Radical 1000 study for you? Your company? Your industry? Read the full report, available for free, at **www.Radical1000.com**

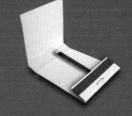

You always have the power
to reinvent your career.
But with that power comes
a significant responsibility:
being accountable for
your own success.

～

CHAPTER
1

DEAL WITH REALITY

WELCOME TO **THE AGE OF**

Remember when our most precious commodities were time and money? Today, there's a new scarcity: life experiences. As the world becomes concentrated, our experiences get crushed to the bare minimum. We try to reduce everything to its essence, extracting every last drop from vacations, time with loved ones, exercise, even private time. At work, deadlines shorten, budgets shrink, expectations rise.

Not everyone will embrace the Age of Intensity, but this is the new reality. And for careerists like you, it creates extraordinary opportunity. Your higher tolerance for stress and appetite for risk allow you to thrive in the chaos. Your multitasking comes in handy when you're downing triple espresso lattes while leading a conference call. *On a cell phone.* **In traffic. DRIVING A STICK.**

INFO TO GO

Want to create more opportunity for yourself, and your company, in the Age of Intensity?
Visit **www.age-of-intensity.com**.

INTENSITY.

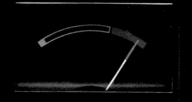

02
REVOLUTION

IS THE NEW STATUS QUO.

Change can make anyone feel anxious. Most people let that anxiety stop them from moving forward. They opt for safety over brilliance, security over satisfaction. They cower under their desks, hoping to avoid the grenades rolling by. Well, those people are about to get a lot more uncomfortable. Change is no longer the exception. It's the rule. The immutable laws of business are dead. Passion and self-direction have become the dominating traits over security, stability, and consistency.

Ladies and gentlemen, the underdog just got promoted to the top of the food chain.

THE AXLE ON THE GRAVY TRAIN IS BROKEN.

Once upon a time, professionals traded skills for money and experience for security. As long as they showed up for work enough years in a row, they could count on that 4% annual raise, summer company picnics, and promotions as scheduled by the corporate staffing chart.

That so-called "security" is out the window. And good riddance! Old-school career models forced professionals into a passive role, telling them how much they'd make, when they'd advance, and what their job description should be. Security came from others, rather than from within.

Today, nothing is guaranteed, and that's a good thing. You're not guaranteed the 4% raise, which means you're also not locked into it. Your job description is longer, which means you can make it bigger. Instead of waiting around for a promotion, you're proactively building the steps of your career.

04

THE TRADITIONAL CAREER PATH WENT OUT WITH GOLD RETIREMENT WATCHES

Gone are the days of blind loyalty and linear hierarchy. Gone are the red power ties and fat expense accounts. Buh-bye, deals sealed on the golf course. So long, tall skinny staffing pyramids. Have fun in the land of archaic business practices, and give our best to the three-martini lunch.

In the Age of Intensity, you control your success. You decide what your future will be. Instead of being evaluated on the basis of passive obedience or corporate benevolence, you operate the levers of your success: your intellectual horsepower, your outlook, your personal brand, and whatever else you bring to the party. NOW. HERE. TODAY.

RADICAL HOW-TO

HOW TO EMAIL LIKE A CONNOISSEUR

Remember that scene in I Love Lucy when bonbons loaded down the conveyor belt faster than Lucy could unload them? Remind you of your inbox? Randy Woodcock, co-founder of IT masterminds Square One Labs, offers these sly tricks for timestacking* with technology:

-Make sure your email device has the exact same format as those sent from your desktop. Outgoing BlackBerry messages automatically say "sent from my BlackBerry" at the bottom—a dead giveaway you're not in the office. Omit this line in the preferences settings.

-Operate your office desktop by remote control no matter where you are with a provider such as GoToMyPC.com, whether in the corner Starbucks or Tahitian Islands.

-If you absolutely cannot afford to go without connectivity, carry two types of cell phones to double your chance of coverage (e.g., one in GSM, and one in CDMA).

*TIMESTACKING: Extracting every bit of capacity from time for maximum efficiency. Über multitasking.

05

- ☐ **QUALITY OF WORK**
- ☐ **QUALITY OF LIFE**
- ☐ **QUALITY OF COMPENSATION**

PICK ONE.

Is your priority to be a rockstar in your industry? Or go home at 5 p.m.? Or have a wheelbarrow full of stock options? They're all valid choices, but no job gives you all three, at least not now. You don't have to choose one to the exclusion of the others, but you do have to prioritize your end goals. Once you know who you are and what you're about, it's easier to focus your time and talents to be happy in your life as a whole.

In the Age of Intensity, being happy in your job is all about finding a company whose priorities are in line with yours. If you're dedicated to exceptional performance, but your company is only dedicated to short-term profits, you and your company do not share the same goals. You're an artisan in a widget factory.

Of course, ultimately, quality of work affords you the ability to choose your schedule, and make a nice salary, and enjoy the glow of knowing you're living as your best self. For me personally, I'm dedicated to quality of work and family time. But as anyone with kids can tell you, those two often seem mutually exclusive. My solution? Start my workday at dawn, and finish by 5 pm. That way I'm not compromising work or family time…only my ability to stay awake for David Letterman.

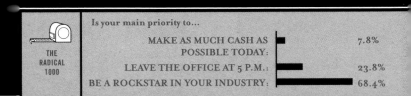

Is your main priority to...	
MAKE AS MUCH CASH AS POSSIBLE TODAY:	7.8%
LEAVE THE OFFICE AT 5 P.M.:	23.8%
BE A ROCKSTAR IN YOUR INDUSTRY:	68.4%

THE RADICAL 1000

BREAK OUT THE NUNCHUCKS AND LET THE STREETFIGHTING BEGIN.

Victories are no longer civilized affairs won by following the rules. Not in the boardroom, and not on the squash court. Today, success is won in the streets with your cunning and instinct. You have to roll up your sleeves. You have to figure out how to get to the sales meeting to present your work, even if all flights out of O'Hare are delayed because of a blizzard.

Are you willing to push harder, work faster, and think smarter no matter what obstacles arise?

Yes?

THEN GET UP OFF THE FLOOR, WIPE YOUR BLOODIED CHIN, AND GET BACK IN THE FIGHT.

DARWIN WAS WRONG.

In chaotic times, everyone focuses on survival. But the fittest don't just survive—they flourish.

If you can thrive even in the craggiest environments, you won't just overcome difficult times. You'll succeed because of them.

Take your lead from a careerist of the animal kingdom: the cockroach. He evolves one step ahead of everyone around. He can survive a week without his head, feed himself for a month from the glue on the back of a stamp, and survive a nuclear blast. Surely you can pull through that all-nighter.

WORK IS HARD.

It just is. As soon as you accept this, you can stop resisting, and start putting your energy into moving forward. The paradox, of course, is that once you're moving forward, work stops feeling so hard.

Everyone looks for shortcuts. But there are no shortcuts. Greatness is never easy, and some days it's not fun. But for careerists, great is the only thing worth being.

INFO TO GO

Are you an emailophile? Do you check email before your first cup of coffee, or sneak in one last email as the plane pulls away from the gate? Read my magnum opus "Ode to Mobile Email." Find it at **www.emailophile.com**, along with plenty of other goodies for the CrackBerry addict.

I YOUR BUSINESS CARD SAYS.
'RE AN ENTREPRENEUR.

orld in which the average job tenure is 3.5 years,
in't allow your company to point you in a direction
ore. (And, really, do you want it to?) Personal security
d come from within. As the CEO of your own career,
lways have the authority to choose your next steps.

ME&Co.

THE
RADICAL
1000

Do big changes make you feel:

STRESSED: 11.4%
EXCITED: 88.6%

AVOID MANUFACTURING BUGGY WHIPS.

The buggy whip trade had a good thing going a hundred years ago. But then a careerist named Henry Ford invented the horseless carriage, and thousands of manufacturers, craftsmen, and salesmen found themselves without a market practically overnight.

So think for a minute. What do you sell? Is your product or service or intellectual property at risk of obsolescence? Are you? Just as you expect your current computer to be obsolete in a matter of years (or months), you should assume your current job description will be out of date eventually. And that's okay, as long as you defend against career stagnation. How? Keep your antennae finely tuned to watch where things are going. Make a point to learn fresh skills. Constantly reinvent yourself, and your company. Re-evaluate what business you're in on a regular basis. Evolve more quickly than your surroundings, so you don't wake up one day and suddenly realize you're manufacturing the Age of Intensity version of buggy whips.

INFO TO GO

Want to reject today's model of success in favor of tomorrow's? Check out **www.buggy-whip.com**

TRANSFORM
OR DIE.

A PARABLE:

The world's fattest man weighed 800 pounds.
Doctors said he had to lose weight. His life depended on
becoming leaner and changing the way he did things.
He didn't. He was buried in a piano case.

The End.

LUCK IS FOR WIMPS.

You don't need a genie's lamp to find your success. Or a horseshoe. Or a rabbit's foot. You already possess everything you'll ever need to succeed. Only by creating opportunity within your circumstances can you actively shape the results. Luck may or may not be on your side, but action is 100% within your control. (That being said, feel free to cross your fingers as well.)

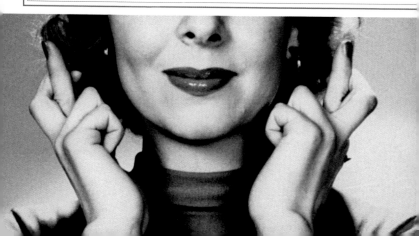

NOW IS THE IDEAL TIME TO TURBOCHARGE YOUR CAREER.

Yes, it's an unpredictable time in business. No question. Uncertainty prowls in every corner. For many of us, the recession was our first taste of our own professional mortality. And while we all feel more comfortable with a few rules in place, every day more rules fall by the wayside.

Amidst this uncertainty, certain careerist traits become more valuable: entrepreneurialism, tenacity, and the resourcefulness to squeeze blood from a turnip.

Three simple ways to boost your long-term equity, market value, and self-worth:

1) Become a smarter employee: find an unexploited niche within your category or company.

2) Build a stronger web of people to support you, inside your workplace and out.

3) Attack undiscovered projects to gain prized exposure and knowledge.

S ALL VERY,
GOOD NEWS
'RE A CAREERIST.

s are custom-built for the chaos of modern
. And modern business is being built, day-by-
careerists.

:s grasp their own power. They understand what's
once they decide to make it so. While everyone else
rates on finding a shortcut and taking the customary
1 can concentrate on what's next in your life.

of scratching your head and wondering how to deal
heaval, invent entirely new ways of operating.
hing blocks you from moving forward on a tradi-
ack (perhaps the job market, or your skill set, or the
/), how can you still be productive?

**, your success has to come from you.
herefore, it belongs to you.**

Your job is one stop
on a journey, not a La-Z-Boy
and bag of cheese puffs.

MASTER THE WORKPLACE

ASPIRE

TO BE THE DUMBEST PERSON IN THE ROOM.

Working with smart people is the mack daddy.
The be-all and end-all. It's the single most important
criterion for evaluating your current or potential job.

What do you do if you're surrounded by myopic clients,
apathetic coworkers, or wussy management?

*1) Find motivating people to collaborate with, people smarter
than you.*

*2) Read articles and books by industry stars to expand
your point of view.*

*3) Plug into people outside your office by attending classes,
workshops, and anything else that will expand your knowledge
and skill base.*

*4) Scram before you become a bitter drone with a big ol'
pile of **trapped equity.***

*TRAPPED EQUITY: Investments of time and effort that you can't take
with you when you leave a job. Example: your batting average on the
company softball team. See also: *indentured servitude.*

16

POLITICS HAPPEN WHEN PEOPLE FEEL INSECURE ABOUT THEIR WORK.

It's an insidious cycle.

When you're prevented from doing your best work, you lose confidence. You look for other ways to differentiate yourself. Maybe you stay late, just for show, or compliment the boss on her hideous new haircut. You get the disquieting impression of being evaluated on something other than performance. Or even worse, you're evaluated on something beyond your control. This cycle of politics distracts from what matters (producing results) and focuses on what doesn't matter (elevator repartee). Between your growing insecurity and budding ulcer, how can you possibly do your best work? (Quick, compliment her new outfit as well.)

The main reason senior executives quit jobs? Internal and external politics. It requires too much intellectual and emotional energy to manage. In smart companies, people advance on the merit of their performance and let the rest take care of itself.

**AGE OF
INTENSITY
SIDEBAR**

THE CLM: CAREER LIMITING MOVE

*Certain mistakes will cut your career off at the knees and make it beg for mercy.
In our Radical 1000 Research, plenty of CLMs were good old fashioned screw
ups like "arguing" and "being late." More poignant were the themes of "staying
at a lame job too long" and "allowing a bad boss to let me think less of myself."*

Watch and learn from these other choice CLMs:

"Xeroxing my resume, and accidentally leaving it
in the machine right before my boss used it."

"Crying while asking for a raise."

"Making a dumb mistake on a simple task for the CEO."

"Getting drunk with co-workers and singing Madonna songs
at the top of my lungs."

"Trashing my boss on emails that he later read."

...and my personal favorite: "Photocopying my butt on the copier
and breaking the glass."

AFTER READING THROUGH HUNDREDS OF CLMs, ONE
THING'S FOR SURE. BEWARE THE OFFICE HOLIDAY PARTY.

INFO TO GO

Ready to confess your most haircurling CLM,
and read ones we couldn't print here?
Log on to **www.forehead-smack.com.**

17

CHAOS UNLOCKS OPPORTUNITY.

When a company reshuffles, or a major player leaves, or an entire industry shifts, uncertainty overthrows the usual structure of hierarchy. Emergencies need solutions. What kind of alchemy* can you perform?

Instead of joining the complaining, stalling, and anxious scanning of the horizon, stop and ask yourself: What's your competitive edge? What can you offer that others can't (or won't)? Can you offer your time, your ideas, your ferocious refusal to give up? Valuable assets, all of them. Never before have people so desperately needed answers, inspiration, and guts.

Transform difficulty into opportunity.

Build lifeboats as the *Titanic* sinks.

---

* ALCHEMY: The process of turning a mediocre situation *(such as a lame job or relationship)* into gold.

(Who better than to comment upon Truth 17 than Number Seventeen, the brilliant design firm for this book?)

Creatively speaking, chaos can be your best friend. We've come up with some of our best ideas under the most chaotic of circumstances: a last minute deadline, a threat, a panicky client. When you have nothing to lose, you're freer to access the more intuitive parts of your brain. The traffic cop of your intellect gets distracted by the chaos, leaving your creative side with nothing but opportunity.

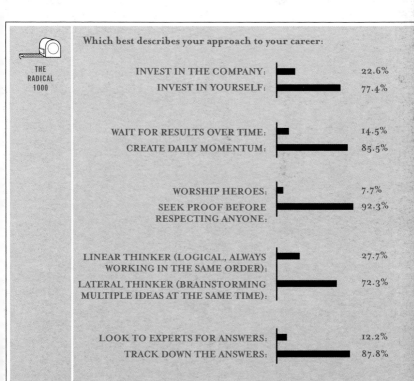

THE RADICAL 1000

Which best describes your approach to your career:

INVEST IN THE COMPANY:	22.6%
INVEST IN YOURSELF:	77.4%
WAIT FOR RESULTS OVER TIME:	14.5%
CREATE DAILY MOMENTUM:	85.5%
WORSHIP HEROES:	7.7%
SEEK PROOF BEFORE RESPECTING ANYONE:	92.3%
LINEAR THINKER (LOGICAL, ALWAYS WORKING IN THE SAME ORDER):	27.7%
LATERAL THINKER (BRAINSTORMING MULTIPLE IDEAS AT THE SAME TIME):	72.3%
LOOK TO EXPERTS FOR ANSWERS:	12.2%
TRACK DOWN THE ANSWERS:	87.8%

18

INVENT OPTION C.

Rarely are you faced with an "A or B" decision, a black-and-white absolute. If you want Option A (e.g., a raise), but your employer wants Option B (more work, and still no raise), it would appear you're at a deadlock. You, however, are a careerist, and as such you have the creativity and moxie to invent Option C. In this case, Option C might be that you expand your scope of duties, but get an additional 2 weeks off plus a car allowance. There are always goodies to put on and take off the table.

REAL DEAL ANECDOTE

CHANGING THE PROBLEM

When space exploration began, there was an insurmountable obstacle. No one could make a material able to withstand the heat of re-entry. The problem seemed unsolvable. Finally, someone had an idea. They stopped looking for a material that wouldn't melt, and focused on finding a way to get the astronauts safely back to Earth. The solution, it turns out, was a shell designed to melt off.

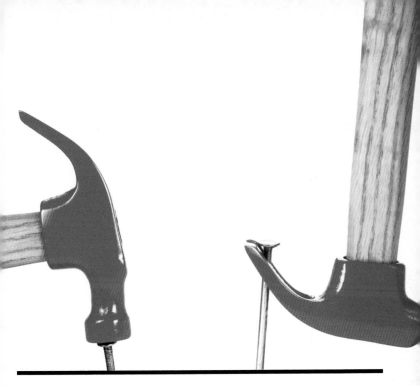

If
you
can't
change
the
solution,
change
the
problem.

19

BEING IN A CRAP JOB ISN'T YOUR FAULT. *STAYING* IN A CRAP JOB IS.

This one hurts and I say it gently. So many people are just trying to survive in their jobs. But here's the thing: Your career belongs to you, and only you. Even in a loathsome job, even if you're paying private school tuition for two kids, you're not without options. A job can control your time and paycheck. But it cannot control your future. Unless you allow it to.

DON'T WORK FOR SOMEONE YOU DON'T RESPECT.

The problem with working for idiots isn't the hair tearing, teeth gnashing, and tongue biting. It's the not-learning part. Unless you're a one-man band, you're a tiny fraction of the overall team. Outstanding results require that everyone, from the interns to the big chiefs, dedicate themselves to the vision.

Is your job as big as you are?

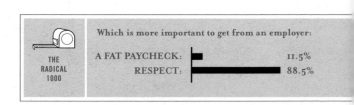

THE RADICAL 1000

Which is more important to get from an employer:

A FAT PAYCHECK: 11.5%
RESPECT: 88.5%

HONOR THE KARMIC CIRCLE.

Remember that whole Golden Rule thing? Whatever you put out there, it will come back to you. Business can get vicious, and the perpetrators almost always self-implode. When you backstab, or eat someone else's lunch out of the office refrigerator, or fib about the delivery dates, you're putting bad energy out there. Integrity, mentoring, acknowledgement, common courtesy—when these principles drive your life, they not only support your career, but also support every single person you come in contact with.

Now please join hands and sing "kum-bay-ya."

OWN

Are you willing to dedicate yourself to a career worth loving? What kind of future could your career help you build? What's stopping you from building it?

⤳

YOUR CAREER

22

OWN YOUR CAREER, OR IT WILL OWN YOU.

Career ownership begins when you start generating capital within yourself. It creates true power: the power to choose how, where, when, and with whom you work. The power to choose your goals, your path, who to be, who not to be. Career ownership allows you to choose your life.

Which has had the greatest influence on your success:

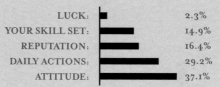

LUCK:	2.3%
YOUR SKILL SET:	14.9%
REPUTATION:	16.4%
DAILY ACTIONS:	29.2%
ATTITUDE:	37.1%

23

YOUR "JOB" IS NOT

These two words used to mean the same thing. But no more. Today your job is where you work: duties, coworkers, office space. A job is a means to an end. A vehicle to get you where you want to go. A career, on the other hand, is the long-term journey. You will probably have many jobs, and probably many professions, all bundled into your single career. Your career represents your holistic professional path. It's the sum total of every idea and action and vision that uniquely comes from you.

Whatever you want (more money, more satisfaction, more time off), keep in mind that your job isn't an end in itself. Your job is a tool. No more, no less.

You can be fired from your job.
But you'll never be fired from your career.

YOUR "CAREER."

**RADICAL
HOW-TO**

HOW TO PLEASE BOTH THE WIFE *AND* THE GIRLFRIEND

How can you make your career AND your job happy at the same time? What can you do today that will contribute not only to your company, but to your own portable equity? One example is to volunteer your time on a juicy project. For instance, proofread all sales proposals or handle pricing. You'll acquire exposure to the best people and the best thinking. You'll get contacts, skills, knowledge, and a new line on your resume. Best case scenario, you'll be identified in the industry as someone who worked on it.

See also Truth 87: Your job description is not your self-description.

YOU ARE YOUR MOST IMPORTANT CLIENT.

So many of us create visions and lead projects, but have little idea of where our own careers are headed. We might spend 60+ hours a week managing a crucial assignment but neglect our own personal career strategies. Approach your own career with no less focus and determination than you would bring to your most promising new business prospect.

Who are you as a professional? What do you stand for? Others can't know if you don't. Create a personal strategy, then use it to drive your thoughts and actions.

REAL-DEAL ANECDOTE

GOD IS IN THE DETAILS

Stonewall Jackson:

One of history's greatest war heroes. Worshipped by the Confederacy, adored by the southern ladies, feared by the Union army, and accidentally killed by his own soldiers.

MAKE BUREAUCRATS NERVOUS.

There's an expression in the technology field, "Nobody ever gets fired for buying IBM." Yeah, well, no one kicks ass by metaphorically buying IBM either. Corporate ideology is fine for the masses, but not for the careerist. In a one-size-does-NOT-fit-all world, the obvious, conventional choice is rarely the most advantageous choice. Opportunity hides in unexpected places.

REAL-DEAL ANECDOTE

MAKING THE MUSIC INDUSTRY NERVOUS
A lone college student named Shawn Fanning overturned the $100 billion music industry. His invention, a little something named Napster, permanently changed how music is bought and sold.

CIRCUMSTANCES CAN'T CRIPPLE YOUR CAREER AS MUCH AS DOUBT OR PASSIVITY.

It's impossible to act powerfully when you feel like a casualty of forces outside of your own control. It can be easy to feel as if the future is determined by the economy, a boss, politics, or even luck. In the face of such fearsome enemies, it's only natural to relinquish control. In truth, the most dangerous enemies of success prowl within ourselves—apathy, uncertainty, complacency. By overthrowing these enemies, you make room for your own progress.

Get out of your own way.

27

WORRY LESS,
DO MORE.

I know. Your brain jumps ahead to the worst-case scenario. As an analytical person, you're used to thinking critically through every possible angle. I hear you. The problem is, focusing on the potential negative is incredibly draining and time consuming. Most of those paranoid scenarios are unrealistic anyway. So much better to put your energy where it can actually do something. Into action.

**You only get a finite number of thoughts.
Choose wisely.**

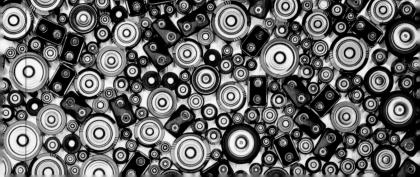

THE MOST RISKY DECISION
IS NOT MAKING ONE.

When you make decisions by default, you relinquish the right to a choice. Not deciding is deciding. Not actively pushing yourself to more ambitious places is leaving the result up to chance. Such a weak place to be.

**ULTRA
CAREERIST
ADVICE**

PHIL KEOGHAN ON RISK

Phil hosts CBS's Amazing Race, and along with coauthor Warren Berger, wrote No Opportunity Wasted: Creating a List for Life. So who better to ask about risk than a guy who goes to the office with man-eating sharks (literally)? Phil's observations on laying it on the line:

- As a society, we've stopped taking risk in our lives. We've started living in fear. We're so busy obsessing over restrictions that we've become scared to fully live.

- You must be prepared to fail if you're ever going to succeed. Otherwise you play it safe, and get stuck protecting what you have.

- Like any muscle, risk requires a certain amount of training. How badly could you want it if you're not willing to put in the hard work?

29

ULTIMATELY, YOU'LL HAVE THE CAREER YOU EARN.

No one will make it happen but you. Period.

AGE OF INTENSITY SIDEBAR

THE CHEESY TREE ANALOGY
(Note: This analogy is cheesy, but sometimes clarity wins out over style.) Imagine your career as a tree trunk. The rewards such as salary or respect are the fruit. Your hard work fertilizes the roots. Without fertilizing the roots, pretty soon you're eating ramen noodles for dinner. And I mean that literally.

INFO TO GO

In the Radical Research 1000, 96% of respondents said they're paid less than they're worth. Are you feeling underpaid too? Go to **www.ramen-noodles-again.com**.

IN VERBS.

Action is the only way to come from a place of strength. Having a meeting about a breakthrough client strategy, or emailing about plans for a terrific management retreat, or swearing you'll stop sneaking Ding Dongs on your low-carb diet—it all means nothing if the idea never comes alive. Spend less energy talking about what could or should get done and more on getting it done.

Okay, enough talking.

ULTRA CAREERIST ADVICE

KEVIN CARROLL, ON LIVING IN PLAY

Imagine this. A young boy. Born to alcoholic parents. Abandoned at age six. Discovers play, then sports. Enters the Air Force. Masters six languages. Joins Nike as an agent for corporate play. Writes a book, "Rules of the Red Rubber Ball." Impossible, right? Meet Kevin.

His advice for play:

-Ask yourself: As a kid, what play obsessed you?

-What kinds of risk-taking and problem solving excited you? Now think.

-How can you inject more of that into your work?

-Every experience, whether an obvious victory or not, makes the next one possible. Find meaning in each one, in order to beget the next.

-Never surrender to circumstances. There's always another path to discover or create.

Genius without action
is worthless.

REJECT MEDIOCRITY

YOU CAN BE COMFORTABLE, OR OUTSTANDING, BUT NOT BOTH.

*What lives outside your comfort zone? Better results?
A more fulfilling career? A more powerful place in the
world? Something bigger than yourself? Once you
decide, the question becomes: Are you willing to go
outside your comfort zone to get it?*

If it's true that 90% of success is just showing up, the other 10% is kicking yourself in the ass to get going. Progress doesn't happen in the comfort zone.

Take a lesson from our friends, the weight lifters. Peak muscle development happens when the muscle is near the point of complete exhaustion. If you're comfortable, you're not done. It's only when you want to stop that you start making progress.

If you want to step it into high gear, be ready to get a little unreasonable. Exceptional results don't happen within standard parameters.

Sometimes you have to go over the top to get to the other side.

RADICAL HOW-TO

HOW TO KICK SERIOUS BOOTIE

The next time you're working on a project and want to deploy your very best, consider these three tiers of expectations:

Delivering: What is expected? For example, getting the proposal to the client on time. (This is where the bulk of people, and companies, will stop. They'll deliver what's expected, and no more.)

Overdelivering: Next, what is desired? For example, including a careful analysis of how your recommended strategy will improve the company's revenue over the next five years. (This is where "overdelivering" comes in; most of your competition stops at this point.)

Expanding beyond: Finally, what is beyond expectations? For example, creating and including samples. (And this, my friend, is where you really shake your groove thang.)

32

IT'S IMPOSSIBLE
TO BE HAPPY
WITHOUT MOMENTUM.

At least, it's impossible for a careerist to be happy without momentum.* If you're stuck in one way or another, soon you'll be frustrated at best, demoralized at worst. Without momentum, you stop growing and start existing.

**INSIDE
HOT TIPS**

WHEN MOMENTUM SLOWS
Stefano Hatfield, senior editor at global newspaper Metro, says it best:
"The time to do radical things is when you're not forced to do them. Make decisions
from a position of strength." His tips for knowing when momentum has slowed:
-When you stop feeling challenged, and start feeling resentful
-When money, perks, and lifestyle become more important than growth
-When you quit fighting for what's right, and settle for what's easiest

*Gentle caveat: "Motion" and "momentum" are two very different things.
Just because you're whipping up a frenzy doesn't mean you're creating
valuable action. Sometimes momentum means staying in the same job,
inventing fresh opportunity.

THE MOMENTUM FORMULA _____

The following formula will help you dramatically improve the direction and speed of your career.

MOMENTUM = GOALS
+ ATTITUDE
+ SKILL SET
+ ACTION
+ NETWORK

Meaning, your career progress is a function of:

Determining what you want

Approaching every task with that goal in mind

Gaining knowledge on how to accomplish something

Getting in motion

Surrounding yourself with people who support you

INFO TO GO

Ready to accelerate your momentum? This online exercise will help your career go from 0 to 60 in breakneck speed: **www.self-induced-whiplash.com.**

WORK ETHIC
TRUMPS TALENT.

Talent is just so terribly glamorous. Talent takes a drag on its cigarette and says nonchalantly, "Oh, that idea? I came up with it in the shower."

On the other hand, there's work ethic. Ugh, work ethic. How tedious.

Talent has sex appeal. By comparison, work ethic is talent's bucktoothed, flat-chested, schoolmarm sister.

But here's the thing. Talent is fickle. Some days it shows up, other days it stays in its bathrobe until noon. You don't even get to choose how much talent you're born with.

Consistent success requires a high level of engagement, tenacity, and optimism.* I've always been a hard worker because if I can't be most talented person in a room, I can still be the hardest working. Is that sexy? Not a bit. Does it work? Absolutely.

Work ethic is the only equal-opportunity resource. Anyone can work hard.

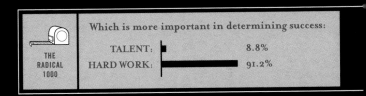

	Which is more important in determining success:	
THE RADICAL 1000	TALENT:	8.8%
	HARD WORK:	91.2%

*Caution: I'm not saying you need to work all the time and not have a life. This isn't about working in a sweatshop or staying at your desk until 2 a.m. It's about giving your best, to be your best.

APPLAUSE IS APPROXIMATELY
.003% OF SUCCESS.

In real life, victories aren't heralded by trumpets, red carpets, cheering crowds or ticker tape parades. In real life, victories happen in the tiniest details of every moment of every day.

ULTRA CAREERIST ADVICE

LIZ PHAIR, SUPERSTAR MUSICIAN/SUPERSTAR CAREERIST

Sure, Liz is famous the world over for her kickass rock and roll. But did you know she's also a careerist extraordinaire? Her advice for a meteoric career:

- Don't be afraid to fail. And when you do fail, ask questions. Sure it's uncomfortable, but if you understand exactly what happened, you can get better and stronger.

- Have a clear sense of what your company wants, so that you can constantly adapt your skills and adjust your game plan.

- No matter what your job title or profession, you are your own business. Your employer is a partner in your career.

- You have so much more power than you think. Don't give it away.

WE EACH HAVE
THE POTENTIAL TO DO
SOMETHING BEYOND OUR
WILDEST IMAGINATION,
AS LONG AS WE'RE PREPARED
TO MAKE IT HAPPEN AT
ANY GIVEN MOMENT
OF OUR LIVES.

BEING A STAR IS PRICE OF ENTRY.

These days, it's expected that you'll be great in your job. Simply meeting standard parameters doesn't impress anyone anymore. The bar is higher than ever before. We've been squeezed into doing more with less. We have to be better, faster. There are fewer jobs, and more talented people to fill them. In the Age of Intensity, anything that's not extraordinary is just plain ordinary.

THE ICON SAYS

"If I'd known I was going to be Pope, I would have studied harder."
—POPE JOHN PAUL II

BEWARE AVERAGE.

Average stalks you at the office, when you'd rather go home. It oozes into your thinking when those around you settle for "good enough." It digs its claws into your reputation. It pollutes your standards and poisons your goals. Average is your archenemy. Quick, before it's too late: Exterminate it.

Choose the fast track.
Choose the third wind.
Choose the red-eye.
Choose the left lane.
But always, always, refuse average.

WATCH THE PLATEAU.

There's a point in many situations when you start settling in, getting cozy. In your job, it's when you get so comfortable with the 9-to-5 that you stop worrying about your next step. When goals stop evolving, they become outdated. But as a careerist, you always have a choice in the matter. Continually re-evaluate according to your ongoing circumstances. When your life stops growing, your spirit starts dying. If you see this plateau, listen to the alarms going off in your head and run screaming from the room.

**A body in motion stays in motion.
A body at rest gets fired.**

**INSIDE
HOT TIP**

"SHOULD I STAY OR SHOULD I GO?"

Is your job paying excellent cash, but forcing you to work crazy hours? Hmm, might be worth it while you pay off that debt—until you can take a job with a smaller paycheck but greater flexibility.

Is your job allowing you to work a 35-hour week but boring you to tears? Might be perfect while you're networking for that new job over apple martinis every evening.

YOU CAN ONLY CONTROL HOW HARD YOU TRY.

You can't control your clients, your coworkers, your boss, the economy, or even when inspiration strikes.

What you are 100% in charge of is how much heart you put into something. At the end of the day, that's all that matters, because that's within your power.

Just grab another iced coffee and revel in the insania.*

AN INDEX OF CAFFEINATION:

Pure caffeine is powdery, white, and addictive. (Hmm.) It boosts the speed of your mental processing, your alertness, even your mood.

Coke: 34 mg
Shot of espresso: 40 mg
Tea: 50 mg
Energy drink 80 mg
Excedrin: 130 mg
Brewed Coffee : 200 mg

Just be sure to save your 400+ mg doses for serious buckle-down days. Otherwise you develop a tolerance, which defeats the whole purpose of chemical acceleration.

Source: *National Geographic,* January 2005

*INSANIA: A jittery, manic high resulting from too much caffeine, adrenaline, and stress.

39

WRITE YOUR MANTRA STATEMENT

You wake up. Roll over. Yawn. As you come alive to your day ahead, what inspires you to get out of bed? Are you excited by prospects ahead, or deadened by the drudgery of minutia on your to-do list? What kind of future are you living into? What is your purpose? The answer lies in your mantra statement.

What's a mantra statement, you ask? Excellent question. You're well acquainted, of course, with a mission statement. Most mission statements use jargonic fluff to state watered-down shareholder goals on a PowerPoint slide. ("We put the Q in Quality!") A mission statement generally speaks purely to rational goals. A mantra statement, on the other hand, reveals the true, underlying purpose. A mission statement lives in your head; a mantra statement lives in both your head and your soul.

HERE'S AN OLD STORY.

> Three bricklayers were working and someone asked, "What are you doing?" The first said, "I'm laying bricks." The second said, "I'm building a straight wall." But the third said, "I'm creating a cathedral for God."

Straight wall = mission statement
Cathedral to God = mantra statement

Think of your own life purpose for a moment. What's your big picture intention? What are you doing with this one and only life of yours?

REAL-DEAL ANECDOTE

When I first started writing this book, I had a mission statement: sell a lot of copies. However, for me personally, selling books feels about as inspiring as laying bricks. So I took a step back, reframed my thinking, and realized that selling books wasn't my underlying purpose. My true goal—my mantra statement—was to help people create careers worth loving. Today, that's what gets me out of bed in the morning. And if I can do that, I figure, the rest will take care of itself.

INFO TO GO

What's your mantra statement? Do you have one? It should define the goal that inspires you on a daily basis. Something that speaks to you. Let's create yours right now.
Go to **www.mantra-statement.com.**

GO FOR NERVOUS.

If your goals are comfortable, they're not big enough. When you start to feel a little twinge in your stomach and moistness on your palms, you're getting close. You don't have to wait until all the pieces are assembled in perfect formation. It's okay to feel nervous about what you're doing; that doesn't make it wrong. In fact, it may just make it right.*

Strap on the cojones and go.

Play like you're not afraid to lose.

*Big honkin' caveat: "Nervous" is not the same as "irresponsible." Don't open the Elephant Housebreaking Company and then call me when you have trouble finding clients.

IF YOU'RE UNHAPPY, CHECK THE WEATHER REPORT.

As careerists, we take responsibility for our actions. However, if you've been feeling seriously discouraged for a while, take a look around. Is the collective self-esteem low? It's entirely possible you're doing everything right, and may be doing better than you realize given the situation. Nothing personal. When the weather changes, your experience will probably change too.

HALF OF ALL PROFESSIONALS ARE BELOW AVERAGE.

It's a bell curve. Becoming even a measly 10% better can take you from a B+ to an A+. Achievers are separated from the masses by the merest fractions, as well as a tolerance for cold pizza. Intimidated? No need. Here's a happy thought: Even the simplest details (showing up on time, writing thank-you notes, following up on calls) put you ahead of the pack.

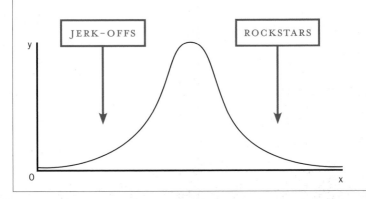

AGE OF INTENSITY SIDEBAR

GRANOLA BARS VS. DING DONGS:
LUNCHTIME IN THE AGE OF INTENSITY

Sometimes, you just have to sit down and jam something out, and there's no time (or budget) for a delivery meal. How can a vendovore* keep going on a diet of Doritos and adrenaline?

-Always include protein. In the vending machine this means peanut butter crackers, sunflower seeds, and corn nuts.

-Balance salty and sweet. My personal favorite: Dump a pack of M&Ms into a hot bag of popcorn. Shake so the M&Ms melt inside their little shells. Mmm.

-With caffeinated beverages, try to sustain the buzz without combusting it with sugar.

*VENDOVORE: Worker who subsists almost exclusively on Cheetos, Bugles, Funyons, and other food in the office vending machine.

WOUNDS HEAL. SCARS FADE. GLORY IS FOREVER.

To kick it into high gear, you have to be a little unreasonable. Exceptional results don't happen within standard parameters. Being in the top percentile in your industry comes with commensurate effort. Careerists are empowered (I dislike that word but it's true) to make our own decisions about our future. Being unreasonable is scary, and that's okay. Only in moving through the fear can you realize your best self. Your top percentile awaits. It's yours to earn.

ULTRA CAREERIST ADVICE

TOM BERNTHAL, ON OPENING A CAN OF CORPORATE WHUP-ASS:

Tom is one of those annoyingly gifted people. Worked at the White House. Then NBC News. Won two Emmys. Then founded Kelton Research at the shriveled age of 27. (Like I said, annoying.) Tom's advice for a bare-knuckle job search:

- During a slow period, practice the surfing effect: Get ready to catch the wave by putting yourself in position, so when it starts you'll get the best ride. Otherwise you're stuck in the sand.

- When companies downsize, and fewer people do more work, stars get promoted more quickly. A decreased staff means more open real estate within a company.

- Remember: employers dislike job searches. They're expensive, time consuming, and exhausting. So seek to meet and impress as many people as possible. When they need someone, if you can circumvent the need for a search, you both win.

Power is
the option
to say no.

COLLECT PORTABLE EQUITY

44

PORTABLE EQUITY IS THE ONLY FORM OF JOB SECURITY TODAY.

In any job, you generate two forms of equity: portable equity and trapped equity.

Portable equity: The reputation you earn. People you meet. Skills you learn. Accomplishments you acquire.

Trapped equity: Your batting average on the company softball team. The time you spend unjamming the printer. Those bagels you bring in for the office.

The difference is this. Portable equity moves with you to your next job. Trapped equity, on the other hand, stays behind.

**INFO
TO GO**

Ready to amass a kingdom of transferable assets?
Visit **www.portable-equity.com**.

Now, I'm not saying that you shouldn't play Sim City with your buddies. I'm just saying that when you're ready to leave a job, portable equity is all that matters. Focus on where you're going as much as what you're doing.

The question is: When you leave your job, what will you have to show for it?

By investing in yourself, you earn more money and kudos. But more importantly, you earn more control over your career, and more options for your life. Portable equity is currency, literally and figuratively. Ultimately, it's more valuable than money or fame—it allows you to do what you love. Not to mention the pleasure of having dozens of horny headhunters drooling over your resume.

OPTIONS = POWER.

Choices translate to more power in your career and your life. Here's an example: Guy A and Guy B work at the same company. Guy A has amassed impressive portable equity; he's a rockstar in his job. He signed up for every sexy project, he built a mondo reputation, and he staked out a unique niche within his industry. He can therefore choose where he works, whom he works with, how much he should earn, and what kinds of projects or clients he accepts.

Guy B, on the other hand, hasn't accumulated portable equity. He's punched in* for the past few years, meeting expectations but not exceeding them. His options are therefore considerably narrowed.

Guy A's portable equity gives him the option to walk away from an unsatisfying situation, the power to choose who he wants to be. That's real power.

*PUNCHING IN: Showing up for work without any sense of intention or purpose. Killing time.

DO YOU HAVE THE
POWER TO WALK AWAY?

THE
RADICAL
1000

Power is:

FAME:	2.8%
MAKING A LOT OF MONEY:	12%
ACCESS TO THE MOST IMPORTANT PEOPLE:	16.3%
THE FREEDOM TO SAY NO:	32.3%
HAVING COMPLETE CONTROL OVER YOUR SCHEDULE:	36.7%

46

MONEY FOLLOWS GREAT WORK, NOT THE OTHER WAY AROUND.

There's an expression: "If you take a job for the money, you always pay." In the long run, the point isn't to make more money. The point is to consistently create work that makes you fulfilled and proud. That's how to reclaim your career.

THE RADICAL 1000	**Consistently throughout our study, we found that what people really want is challenging work, a supportive supervisor, respectful colleagues, and the promise of growth.**

Which would you choose:

A JOB I HATE BUT MAKE THREE TIMES THE MONEY I DO NOW:	13%
A JOB I LOVE AND MAKE HALF THE MONEY I DO NOW:	87%

Which is your idea of professional hell:

LONG HOURS:	3.8%
LOW PAY:	4.7%
BEING MICROMANAGED:	15.6%
DISPRESPECTFUL BOSS OR CO-WORKERS:	75.9%

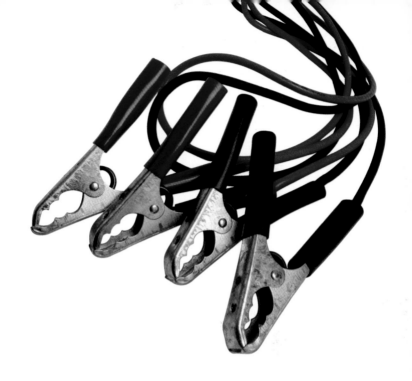

"IS THAT OPPORTUNITY KNOCKING? OR THE REPO MAN?"

*These questions will help you intelligently evaluate a prospect before starting
a bargain basement sale.*

**INSIDE
HOT TIPS**

-Is this an "I'd-sell-my-firstborn" opportunity? Is it a primo company,
with visionary plans, and brilliant co-workers? Are you being offered
greater control and potential?

-If the job isn't well paying, is it inversely rewarding you in other ways?
It's a sliding scale. The less money there is, the greater the opportunity
must be to justify it.

-Are you just giving away the milk for free? Is it an investment, or charity?
Is this offer fair, or just a bunch of cheap bastards low-balling you?

47

RESULTS + REPUTATION + NETWORK

In most careers, income is generated by three things: the work you do, the people you know, and the brand you've created for yourself. Happily, all three are within your control. Boost these three factors, and employers will start getting in line to woo you.

Of course, if your results, reputation, and market value add up to less than what you're paid, then you're in a vulnerable position. Back in the drunken dot–com days, vice president titles were liberally sprinkled among new graduates as a form of recruitment. After the crash, when those VPs went job hunting, guess what? They weren't really VPs. The flashy titles were superficial decorations. It was a false economy. Those pseudo leaders lacked a track record to prove they could do the job, connections to find opportunities, and references to back it all up.

Conversely, you could be working in a low-paying job completely devoid of glamour or bonuses or perks, yet be racking up market value hand over fist. Market value and current compensation are two different things. At the extreme, think of all the people willing to work for Donald Trump for free, because they get all three of the above.

= *YOUR MARKET VALUE*

PEOPLE
YOU KNOW

WORK
YOU DO →   ← YOUR
                     BRAND

CASH COW

THE
RADICAL
1000

Which is most important in determining
someone's market value:

RESULTS YOU'VE PRODUCED:	30.8%
WHO YOU KNOW:	33%
YOUR REPUTATION IN YOUR INDUSTRY:	36.2%

4 8

OPPORTUNITY IS A MORE VALUABLE CURRENCY THAN CASH.

In many industries, you don't get serious money AND portable equity. A job might offer a stellar group of coworkers, glamorous work, and a high-wattage company for your resume. There's only one small detail missing: money. Instead of compensating you with cash, these jobs often compensate you with a different currency: opportunity.

For this reason, boosting your salary might first require a pay cut. Ouch, right? Easier said than done.* Approach it as a strategic investment in yourself, rather than a loss. (Within reason of course. The bank does like to get those credit card payments.)

There are many ways to improve your work, your income, and yourself, and I encourage you to sacrifice as little as necessary along the way.

*Just so you know, I'm no hypocrite. I once took a 50% pay cut in exchange for a U-Haul full of portable equity.

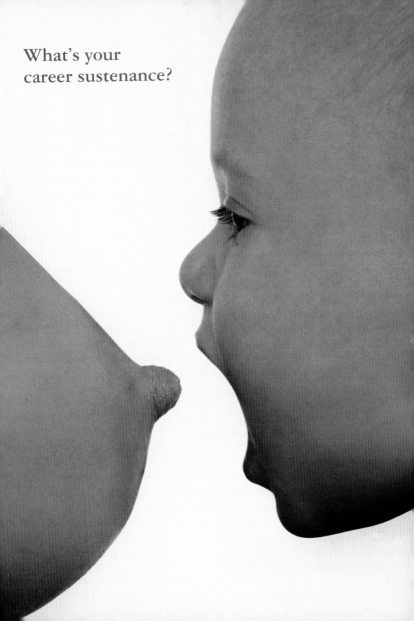

What's your
career sustenance?

YOU ARE YOUR OWN BEST 401(k).

You are the most profitable investment you can make in your own future. Relatively small sacrifices now pay massive dividends in the future.

ULTRA CAREERIST ADVICE

CATHY GRIFFIN ON MARKET VALUE

As a premier consultant and executive recruiter, Cathy deals with some of the hottest and highest–ranking executives around. Her advice for proactively managing your own market value:

-Don't assume your company is going to figure your career out for you.

-Develop your own personal "board of advisors," people who can give you ongoing and accurate input on your situation and yourself.

-Constantly re-evaluate your situation within the immediate context. What worked for you five years ago won't necessarily work now. You've changed, and the market's changed.

-Activate your network of contacts: manage it, expand it, build it, re-think it. Don't let names rot in your Rolodex.

50

CONCENTRATE ON LONG-TERM GOALS OVER SHORT-TERM BOTTOM LINE.

Remember how in college, the choicest internships usually had the lowest pay and the longest hours? But those opportunities offered the best springboards to the next level. That logic still applies. Keep that mindset, focusing on what's next, and next, and next.

If a crap company offers you an extra 25% salary but 50% less portable equity, yeah, you can increase your immediate income by a few more grand. But you'll lessen your chances of retiring early.

THE ICON SAYS

"It is too early to tell."
(CHINESE LEADER ZHOU ENLAI'S RESPONSE IN 1972, WHEN ASKED HIS THOUGHTS ON THE 1789 FRENCH REVOLUTION)

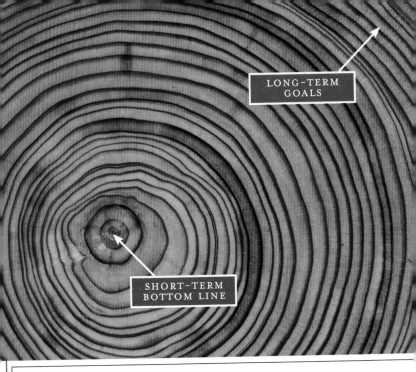

LONG-TERM GOALS

SHORT-TERM BOTTOM LINE

ULTRA CAREERIST ADVICE

ANTHONY von MANDL ON THE LONG-TERM

Once upon a time, Anthony was an entrepreneur with such dedicated vision that he downgraded into a basement apartment to meet payroll. Today his creation, Mike's Hard Lemonade, has outsold every brewer in America and created a new beverage category. Anthony's advice for building long-term growth:

-Lasting growth requires sacrifice. That might mean growing more slowly, or turning down opportunities, or avoiding business partners who don't share your core values.

-Don't pursue growth for the sake of growth. Never value stock price over the experience of your brand.

-There <u>will</u> be times when it feels like you're sinking in quicksand. What pulls you out is your long-term vision, and your employees' shared sense of purpose. You have to stand for more than financial gain.

51

INDECISION GENERATES ANXIETY.

You know when you're on vacation in a foreign city, standing on a street corner, unsure exactly which way to go? Suddenly you start snipping at your travel mates. Doubt feels uncomfortable. My family calls this "tourist indecision."* You're irritated because no one knows which way to go.

Same goes for business. If you're a leader in your company, be aware that indecision generates stress among your staff. When people don't know their next step, they get stuck, then anxious, then negative. Make a decision. Go.

See also Truth 32: It's impossible to be happy without momentum.

*TOURIST INDECISION: Anxiety resulting from a sense of being lost or proceeding without clear direction.

IT'S NICE
TO BE IMPORTANT,
BUT MORE IMPORTANT
TO BE NICE.

This almost-admonition sits framed on the hostess stand
of a frou-frou Beverly Hills restaurant. How great is that?
In other words, congratulations on being a bigwig. Now
please turn around and wait your turn.

Really, the simplest lessons your mother taught you still
apply. Say please. Don't yell. Listen. Write thank-you notes.
Smile. Give hugs as allowed within any given sexual
harassment policy.

See also Truth 21: Honor the karmic circle.

Need a little help with your modern business behavior?
Please visit **www.please-and-thank-you.com**.
Thank you.

**INFO
TO GO**

53

DON'T FOCUS ON YOUR JOB TO THE DETRIMENT OF YOUR CAREER.

Don't give your job so much of your intellectual and emotional energy that you don't have any left for your career. It's easy to get so focused on the minutiae of today's to-do list that you lose sight of long-term plans. But when your day is crammed with putting out fires ("I have to do the PowerPoint deck") you can forget your long-term vision. ("I want to move into a job without PowerPoint decks.") It's difficult to stay true to your goals. Then you wake up in a few years with no job, no equity, and less market value than you started with. In the midst of the daily onslaught, remember where you're headed, and what it's all for.

Caution: Do not be a *gig gigolo*,* bouncing between jobs. That being said, when you support your company, you deserve to be supported by it. In today's economy, without the luxury of job security and guaranteed annual raises, that's only fair.

*GIG GIGOLO: A job whore. Someone who promiscuously switches employment without consideration for their company or future.

GOLDEN HANDCUFFS
BECOME IRON SHACKLES.

Sure, being overpaid sounds nice. Who wouldn't want an extra zero on their salary? But the reality is, if you aren't generating the value to back that salary up, you're in a vulnerable position. When an employer is not just your boss but your only possible meal ticket, you begin to resent him or her. You and the boss both know that you're powerless. You're an indentured servant.*

When you've amassed enough portable equity to leave a dead-end job, there isn't the same feeling of desperation. You're on equal footing. You stay because you choose, not because you're stranded without options. What a better place to be.

*INDENTURED SERVITUDE: Being trapped in a mediocre job because you lack the portable equity to leave in a position of strength.

55

NEVER ALLOW THE SIZE OF YOUR MORTGAGE TO EXCEED THE QUALITY OF YOUR WORK.

It's dangerously shortsighted to drive your career decisions by your cost of living. Eventually, you're trapped without options in a job you might not even want.

Is it a coincidence that a cul-de-sac is also a dead end?

AGE OF INTENSITY SIDEBAR

YOUR JOB'S CRAP: CHERRY RATIO
What is your company costing you, versus providing you? How's your
ratio of cost: benefit? Effort: achievement? Frustration: fulfillment?
Disappointment: delight?

Being happy in your job requires that the good outweigh the bad.
A job can have loads of crap (tight deadlines and low pay), but still be
a good job if it has a good supply of cherries (acknowledgement and
opportunity).

For me, cherries are momentum, a continuous learning curve, cool
opportunities, smart clients, autonomy, positive reinforcement, and
time with my family. What's non-negotiable for your happiness at
work? If you're not getting those things, can you create them? Can you
get them outside of work? On the flipside, what are you absolutely not
willing to put up with? A disrespectful environment? Micromanaging
boss? Kenny G on your officemate's radio (all day)?

Bottom line: A "dream job" is more like a nightmare if it requires a
fistful of Prozac to tolerate.

LEAD

This chapter goes
out to you:
The head honcho.
The bigwig.
Le Grande Fromage.

CHAPTER
6
FROM WITHIN

BE WHERE YOU WANT OTHERS TO GO.

What's your vision for your employees and your company? Are you embodying that vision?

It's called "leading" because you do it from the front.

YOU ARE NOT DONE PAYING YOUR DUES.

Neither am I. We never will be. Mediocrity is tenacious; the second we stop fighting it, we become one of those lurking cronies who wake every morning terrified of getting fired because someone younger, smarter, and cheaper has just mailed in their resume.

The goal here, of course, is not to pedal faster in the rat race. It's to earn the comfort of sitting back one day, and looking back on your career knowing you gave your best, you contributed to others, and you have the rest of your life ahead to feel satisfaction in a job well done.

A CAMEL IS A HORSE
DESIGNED BY COMMITEE.

Horses are graceful, inspiring, and passionate. Camels are practical, efficient, and soulless. Camel ideas often make sense on paper, but they're lumbering in application. Avoid bureaucracy that turns ideas into camels.

**AGE OF
INTENSITY
SIDEBAR**

WHEN SMART COMPANIES GO DUMB

We all do it: become too entrenched in bureaucracy, or make shortsighted decisions at the cost of long–term goals. Has your company unwittingly begun accepting the unacceptable? Signs your smart company may be going dumb:

- Spending thousands on headhunter fees, but forgetting to budget $1 for that employee's birthday card

- Shelling out $2,000 for plane tickets, then cutting back on microwave popcorn

- Treating a computer virus as an emergency, and diseased morale as status quo

**INFO
TO GO**

Want to learn more ways that smart companies go dumb, and how to prevent it? Go to www.blind-spot-idiocy.com.

BUILD, DON'T MAINTAIN.

There are two kinds of people: builders and maintainers.

Builders are most comfortable creating, changing, growing, developing. Maintainers prefer to preserve the existing state of affairs.

Both personality types are necessary in an organization, but leaders are builders. In an organization, status quo is death. If you're not moving forward, you're moving backwards.

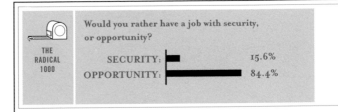

THE RADICAL 1000

Would you rather have a job with security, or opportunity?

SECURITY: 15.6%
OPPORTUNITY: 84.4%

With each success, you risk becoming a little fatter and a little happier. You stop being the scrappy, feisty underdog, and start facing a far more insidious obstacle: stagnancy. Only by relentlessly acting as if you have something to prove can you avoid getting bloated and lazy.

Whatever your success, stay scrappy. Stay agile. Stay hungry. Otherwise, your best practices become a cinderblock chained to your feet as you drop into a chasm of complacency.

REMAIN AN UNDERDOG.

See also Truth 46: Money follows great work, not the other way around.

BE SOMEONE'S HERO.

Once upon a time, someone gave you a piece of advice, or an interview, or an internship, and it became the support you needed to become a careerist. (And just look at you now!) Now it's time to return the favor. Mentor someone. Help them become who they want to be. No, it doesn't have to take a lot of time. And no, you shouldn't wait until you're a grizzled, silver-haired veteran to start.

A good rule of thumb: Support two people for every one that's supported you.

INFO TO GO

Ready to earn some major brownie points? Offer your advice to aspiring careerists in our mentorship forum. All mentors and mentees welcome. Go to: **www.wind-beneath-my-wings.com**.

ONGOING PANIC
KILLS INNOVATION.

Busting it to get something out the door is one thing.
But watch out when people feel a sense of dread every time
you walk in the room. They become flooded. "Heads down
everyone—the boss is coming!" The reek of fear fills the hall.
In the face of short-term panic, people lose vision.

In fact, for most people, the fear of getting fired feels worse
than actually getting fired. When confronted with constant
panic of losing their job, people lose morale, confidence and,
most importantly, the ability to be their best.

Success requires knowing the target, the rules, and the areas to avoid. Without that, it's extremely difficult to focus energy effectively. When the rules keep changing (or aren't established), you spend more time adjusting course than moving forward. It's hard enough to create exceptional results without wasting energy on a snipe hunt. Get clear agreement on the rules and target goals from all decision makers involved.

Performance reviews are a great example of how direction and feedback can proactively steer the course. Honest feedback, both positive and negative, is meaningful when delivered from a place of support. Everyone who works under me knows exactly where the bar is, what the rewards are, and where they are in the game.

IT'S EASIER TO WIN ON THE RIGHT PLAYING FIELD.

RADICAL HOW-TO

HOW TO GIVE A GOOD PERFORMANCE REVIEW

A manager's job is to support every team member in playing at his or her best. How?

When an employee's performance requires hardcore criticism, carefully consider the best way to articulate it with a velvet fist*. A tough performance review has the power to break someone's spirit if thoughtlessly delivered. It also has the power to dramatically improve someone's performance. You, as the manager, are personally responsible for determining which is the result. Unless you're planning to fire the employee, it's crucial you make it clear that the critique has a purpose: helping them play at the top of their game. Give very specific examples, then specific resources for solutions.

In the Age of Intensity, waiting a year for a performance review is about 11 months too long. I recommend an informal review after one month of employment. Start the trajectory in the right direction.

Don't just talk. Listen. Ask questions. Examples: What are your favorite parts of your job? Your least favorite? What's keeping you from being better? Why do your expense reports include receipts from a taxidermist?

*VELVET FIST: Brutally hard information or opinions cushioned by a delicate delivery.

BREED RADICAL CAREERISTS.

Careerists are the most crucial members of any organization.

Why?

They have:

1) *Idealism to see what's possible*
2) *Thought leadership to generate ideas*
3) *Creativity to develop fresh options*
4) *Vitality to inspire others*
5) *Confidence to stand for what they believe*
6) *Assertiveness to fully engage*
7) *Finely-tuned "social antennae" to understand their environment*

If your company is going to flourish beyond your leadership, careerists are the ones who will do it. Identify them, nurture them, and then give them the space to do what they do best.

INSIDE HOT TIPS

STEVEN WILHITE, ON CORPORATE CAREERISTS

How's this for a cool job title: SVP of Global Marketing for Nissan Motors. That's Steve. Respected by colleagues and employees alike for his motivating management style, Steve offers the following tips for boosting employee performance:

-The best leaders hire the smartest, most aggressive people possible, provide them with strategy and parameters, and then get out of the way. Too often, managers squash bright young talent, fearing they'll stir controversy or eclipse the manager's spotlight.

-Seek out people who can offer fresh thinking, even if it's uncomfortable. Without them, there's no ability to change, and no new growth opportunities.

-Every company is critically dependent on having certain people in the organization who are perfectly comfortable being fired for what they believe in. Without conviction and passion, the employee is merely earning a paycheck, and the company is not being challenged to deliver higher performance to a higher level of expectations.

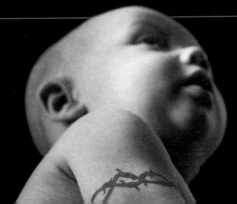

EUTHANIZE
THE DOGS
AND PONIES.

When preparing for a big meeting, I'm all for a tight presentation format. The downfall is focusing on showmanship to the detriment of thinking. Sloppy logic isn't any more impressive just because it's in a pretty typeface. Instead of picking out eight kinds of pastries, find eight more ways your project will drive revenue for the client.

TAKE PEOPLE WITH YOU.

As you grow upward, pull everyone around you up too. When you support the people under your management rather than competing with them, they'll make you shine even brighter. When people recognize their own value, they increase it.

Nicole Williams, founder of Wildly Sophisticated Media, describes this as coming from a place of abundance. She says, "Being a careerist can get lonely. So surround yourself with people you can support, and be supported by. There's enough opportunity in this world to go around."

As any HR manager will tell you, this isn't just for warm 'n' fuzzy reasons. A company's most valuable resource, when you include the investment of recruiting, training, intellectual property, replacement, and client consistency, is its people.

See also Truth 21: Honor the karmic circle.

Some days, success is about luck,
or talent, or skill. But most days, success
is about wrestling failure to the ground
until it screams uncle.

CHAPTER
7
FAIL SUCCESSFULLY

49

MISTAKES
ARE TUITION.

My mother has an exquisite gift for finding value in negative situations. When I made mistakes as a kid (like, daily), she would say, "Well look at that, you just paid tuition. Now you can do it better next time." Such an empowering interpretation of failure.

I've paid some steep tuition in my day. Bigger goals have the higher potential for failure. If you don't experience failure, odds are you're not truly putting yourself out there, taking risks and fully engaging. The trick isn't to avoid failure, but to know how to cope with failure when it does happen.

THE MOST POWERFUL CATALYST FOR SUCCESS
IS FAILURE.

Sometimes, failure is the best thing that could occur. That's when the greatest breakthroughs happen.

Numerous studies show that difficulty during childhood, such as depression or war, often blossoms into success later in life. Difficulty creates a heartier, more resilient approach to survival. In hard times, we either become damaged, or strengthened. Adversity teaches crucial lessons. (How's that for the ultimate silver lining?)

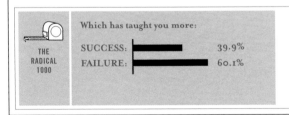

THE RADICAL 1000

Which has taught you more:

SUCCESS: 39.9%
FAILURE: 60.1%

WORK TOWARD *THE POSITIVE,* NOT AWAY FROM *THE NEGATIVE.*

YOU

FAILURE

FEAR CAUSES PARALYSIS.

When someone points a gun at you, you're more likely to stare at the gun than at your potential escape routes. It's instinct. Professional fear works the same way. You freeze, and stare at the problem instead of the myriad of potential solutions.

THE ANTIDOTE TO
FEAR IS ACTION.

Action is the only way to come from a place of strength. By exercising your choices, you reclaim control, and get moving again.

EXAMINE YOUR OWN INTERNAL ISSUES BEFORE BLAMING EXTERNAL PROBLEMS.

It's so easy to blame the office, the boss, the client. And they may very well be at fault. But think for a moment (and be excruciatingly honest):

A) *Is there something you're doing that's causing the problem?*

B) *Is there something you're NOT doing that's causing the problem?*

The more responsibility you can take, the more power you can reclaim in the situation.

LOSE EARLY.

Whenever possible, make losing your decision, something you choose. Not something forced upon you. If it becomes obvious that your task is absolutely doomed, lose sooner rather than later. For example, if it's immediately clear that a new job won't work out because the company is plunging downhill, your division is hemorrhaging clients, and your boss is a schmuck, don't passively wait around, wondering if the situation will change. In this case, inertia is career suicide.

See also Truth 19: Being in a crap job isn't your fault. Staying in a crap job is.

AGE OF INTENSITY SIDEBAR

Are you about to be (gulp) fired? A quick tally of signals that you may be asked to leave soon:

You're not included in meetings

You're given only low-profile assignments

You're not able to look back over the past year and see milestone achievements

There's a pink slip in your mailbox

PULL RABBITS OUT OF HATS, EVEN WHEN THERE ARE NO RABBITS AND NO HATS.

Rarely will you have the resources, tools, training and support necessary to succeed. In fact, you can pretty much count on success seeming like an impossibility. This does not mean it's an impossibility. If it were easy, everyone would do it.

Being the underdog either shuts you down or calls you forth to perform at the highest possible level. How do you respond?

THE ICON SAYS

"The hard is what makes it great."
—TOM HANKS

PROTECT HOPE AT ALL COSTS.

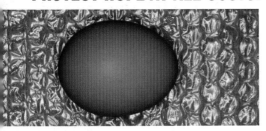

There is something worse than losing your job, reputation, nest egg, or even your pride: losing hope. The whole point of careering is to create a position of strength. Taking a pay cut, trying and failing, committing a CLM—all these can be reversed. But once your hope dies, it's very, very hard to get it back.

REAL-DEAL ANECDOTE

When I was unemployed and on bed rest and losing hope, I leaned on my very wise friend Caskey.

One afternoon I said in despair,
"I just want to get back to my old self!"

To this day I treasure her response. She said:
"You'll never get back to your *old self*.
You're going forward to your *new self*."

INFO TO GO

When the discouragement is almost more than you can bear, visit **www.long-live-optimism.com**.

CAREERISTS ARE HARDEST HIT BY FAILURE.

We distinguish ourselves by our ability to take action and generate results. Ironically this can work against us when we hit a low, because we assume we can pull ourselves out. Numerous studies show that achievers become clinically depressed far more so than the average worker, because they expect so much more of themselves—yet are least likely to seek help.

If you're in a dark phase, remember this. Sometimes progress is internal, and therefore invisible. While it might feel like you're mired in grueling defeat, in fact you're in a chrysalis* phase, preparing to emerge stronger and wiser.

See also Truth 67: Mistakes are tuition.

*CHRYSALIS: A state of change during which your development isn't obvious to the naked eye, but which ultimately results in a dramatic transformation.

EXPECT PEOPLE TO SAY YOU CAN'T MAKE IT.

Careerists have high aspirations, and clock-watchers will drag you down. But don't let anyone cram you into a smaller, less ambitious reality. When someone says you can't do something, learn everything you can from their reasoning. Then tell them to turn around and get back to darning socks.

WALK THE FINE LINE BETWEEN FEELING INSPIRED AND TERRIFIED.

Careerists live by
what's possible,
instead of being confined
by what is.

〜

CHAPTER
8

REINVENT YOURSELF

DO WHAT YOU'D RATHER BE DOING.

Life's too short to slog through a job that's less than inspiring. Would you rather be doing something else? Starting today, envision the process required to meet your goals, then begin to take steps toward your goal.

Researchers at the University of Chicago once divided a basketball team into two groups. One group practiced their drills every day in the gym. Another group did not practice in the gym at all, but spent an equal amount of time visualizing the same drills. At the end of six weeks, the performance of the two groups was indistinguishable.

RADICAL HOW-TO

HOW TO PRY OPEN THE BACKDOOR
Trying to reach someone within a company?
Email can be more effective than a letter or phone call, since people can respond more quickly. Give the email a clear subject header.
If you want to contact Jim Smith but can't find his email address, look on the company's site for other email addresses (e.g., "Human Resources is jsmith@company.com")

FIGURE OUT WHAT'S STOPPING YOU, THEN DEAL WITH IT.

Enough said.

ULTRA CAREERIST ADVICE

SPRINTS VS. MARATHONS

Ginny Hopkirk helps lead footwear design at a quintessential careering company: Nike. Her advice on the difference between a sprint (e.g., a short-turnaround project) and marathon (e.g., a long-term initiative):

-Sprints require an intense burst of extreme focus, and demand your best efforts immediately. Avoid burnout from too many sprints.

-Marathons have sections to gauge and adjust progress.

-Be tenacious, dig deep, tap into your sheer will. Crosstrain your strengths in both.

DON'T LET THE WINDOW OF OPPORTUNITY SLAM SHUT

ON YOUR FINGERTIPS.

Opportunity, by definition, has a limited timeframe.
If an unusual possibility presents itself, don't wait
around to make a decision.

REAL-DEAL ANECDOTE

Comfort for parents of dropouts everywhere: Bill Gates
left Harvard early because he was so convinced that the
timing was perfect for some hair-brained scheme called
a personal computer.

SESAME BEEF

BUCK ROUTINE.

We all have comfortable patterns. I like my Blockbuster night as much as the next guy. But sometimes, habits can insidiously define our lives.

What are you taking for granted, instead of pushing yourself to find a fresher, better solution? Do you always solve problems with the same tactics? Eat lunch with the same group? Sleep on the same side of the bed? Stop digging ruts, and use the shovel to fill them back in instead. Break the conventions of your life. Order something other than kung pao chicken.

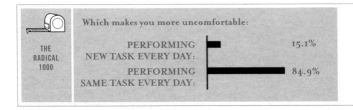

	Which makes you more uncomfortable:	
THE RADICAL 1000	PERFORMING NEW TASK EVERY DAY:	15.1%
	PERFORMING SAME TASK EVERY DAY:	84.9%

IT'S NEVER

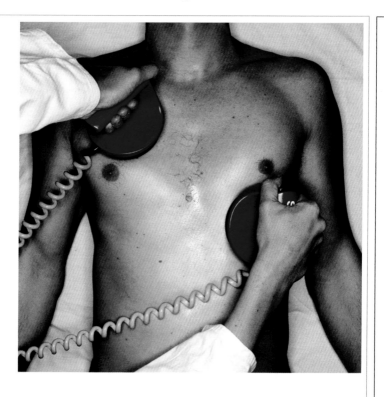

TOO LATE TO START CAREERING.

Sure, it's not easy. And it might require a pay cut. But I've seen it happen many times. What comes out of mid-life careering isn't just renewed earning potential and career velocity, but a much, much happier person. If you're in a job that's less than you are, remember this.

You deserve to have exactly the job you want, no matter how daunting it seems, or how discouraged you feel.

See also Truth 45: Options = Power

"Do one thing every day that scares you."
–ELEANOR ROOSEVELT

THE ICON SAYS

DEMORALIZED IS NOT THE SAME AS DISEMPOWERED.

Let's turn the house lights down for a minute.

There may be times in your career when you feel lost, overwhelmed, beaten down, or even depressed. Right now may even be one of those times. In this situation, careering feels totally unrealistic; it's tough to go boldly when you're trapped in survival mode. I know. But just because you feel powerless doesn't mean you are.

You always have options.
Always.
Always.
Always.

And options, as you know, equal power.
Please keep that in mind when you're tempted
to slit your wrists with a paper clip.

SCREW RATIONAL.

You can't become truly exceptional by coloring within the lines. You just can't. By definition, rules outline a standard path. If you want to exceed standard results, you have to go outside the norm. Rules are limits.

REAL-DEAL ANECDOTE

FAKE FEET AND BIRTHDAY CAKE.

Here's where screwing rational can go wrong. In my last job I got about 50 resumes a week, and people found some rather, err, "interesting" ways to get my attention.

- Before I had a website, someone bought www.sallyhogshead.com and wouldn't give it back until I interviewed him.

- Someone else sent a chocolate sheet cake with his resume digitally printed on the frosting.

- And finally, the grand master daddy: A first-time job hunter sent a fake foot to get her "foot in the door." Um, don't.

85

JUMP, AND A NET
WILL APPEAR.

I've repeated this to myself many a time. It's impossible to be successful when you cling to obsolete situations out of fear. Only when you put yourself out there wholeheartedly can the best opportunities present themselves.

What's your lifelong passion? If you've done your homework and decided what you want to do, then clearly and rationally start building your net. Please note: I'm not suggesting you jump before you're ready. Just don't not do it because you're afraid.

A checklist for jumping:

1) You loathe the idea of going to work in the morning.

2) You're more focused on surviving than flourishing.

3) You've traded the goal of doing your best work for making the boss happy.

4) You've lost faith in the people you work with.

5) You've lost respect for the company.

6) You've lost confidence in yourself.

7) You've stolen a closet full of office supplies and they're on to you.

HOW TO JUMP, BY SABRINA ROSS LEE

Sabrina and I went to Duke together, and let me tell you, Sabrina is one of the most intelligent people I've met. After graduating at the top of her class, she was immediately pulling down serious cash. But after a few years, she decided she wasn't fulfilled. Did she go back to law school? No. Business school? No. Med school? No. She quit her glitzy corporate job and joined a modern dance company. Sabrina's advice for leaping into the unknown:

- Never look down. Jumping is about making the audience momentarily forget gravity exists. That requires, for an instant, refusing to even consider the ground.

- Decide how high you want to jump BEFORE you take off. Once you're in the air, it's already too late.

- To find out how high you can jump without falling, you must first fall. You must push yourself beyond your limits. Rehearsal is all about falling, so that you can precisely calculate your risks.

Do you live to work,
or work to live?

BALANCE
WITH
INTENTION

"BALANCED" IS NOT THE SAME AS "HALF-ASSED."

"Balance" is not an excuse for sneaking out of work early. It's not about being 50/50—it's about being 100/100. You can be fully engaged in your career and making things happen without having a whacked-out personal life. Commit to both with passion. The trick is to be fully invested in whatever you're doing.

ULTRA CAREERIST ADVICE

STEVE STANFORD ON THE 100/100 BALANCE

Named one of TIME's most innovative people of the 20th century, Steve has seriously intense CEO pressures. Yet Steve refuses to compromise his most important job description: Daddy to three girls. Steve's advice on balancing work and family:

- Focus on the long-term goal, not the process. As long as you're progressing toward the goal, you can design a process that works for you.

- Rarely is something so important that it can't wait an hour. People, especially in corporate environments, tend to manufacture an unnecessary sense of urgency.

- In the long run, balance isn't about giving up work or family; it's about reorienting your schedule. Take the red-eye, wake up at 4 a.m., or do whatever it takes to tuck your kids in at bedtime.

YOUR *JOB DESCRIPTION* IS NOT YOUR *SELF-DESCRIPTION*.

As careerists, we're frequently guilty of defining ourselves by our careers. When we get acquainted at a cocktail party, our first question is usually, "So what do you do?" No wonder we personalize our successes and failures.

Defining yourself by your job is fine when it's all going well, because then you're defined as someone who is a valued, productive and rewarded person. The problem comes when you lose the glam job, or decide to take a pay cut, or jump off the corporate treadmill to stay home with your kids. In that case, if you've always defined yourself by your job, the change can assault your self-image.

Try this one for size. Do you insist on living fully, passionately, wholeheartedly? Then you are not your job. Your job is an expression of you…the very best version of you.

HELLO
my name is

ARCHITECT

WORK IS A TWO-WAY STREET.

There's an insidious myth. It says, work is a necessary evil to be tolerated before escaping to "real" life. Your job sucks energy. Your boss is a slumlord and rent is due. In general, work is a "have to," not a "want to."

I think that's pathetic.

I say, work should contribute in direct proportion to its demands. We give time and energy, and in return, we deserve support and excitement. Acknowledgement and respect. New challenges, new skills, new opportunities.

Workers today spend 60 to 70% of our waking hours at work. We owe it to ourselves to create a career deserving of that time. If your work doesn't give as much as it takes, you're missing out on the passion and self-expression of a joyful career. Time to change either what you do, or how you do it.

It's because work demands so much of us that we must demand as much in return.

A JOB WON'T LOVE YOU BACK.

Even if you adore your job, your officemates, your clients, don't invest your entire emotional well-being into work. Don't look to work for the kind of emotional gratification that you should be getting from family and friends.

I've made some bad trade-offs for work by not creating balance. I missed my son's first birthday, his first steps. One day when Quinton was three, he said, "You're not my mommy. You're the office's mommy." Ohhh. That hurts my heart to think about. But from that moment on, I changed my schedule. I don't want to be the office's mommy ever again.

INFO TO GO

Read "Recovering from Workaholism: A 12-Step Program" at **www.workaholics-anonymous.com**.

MAINTAIN HEALTHY RELATIONSHIP HYGIENE.

In many jobs, it's tough not to take office calls during dinnertime with loved ones, or to continually bag out on friends for work. But it contaminates your relationships, and it's difficult to cleanse. Set aside time to engage wholeheartedly with those human beings you call friends and family. Find the off-switch.

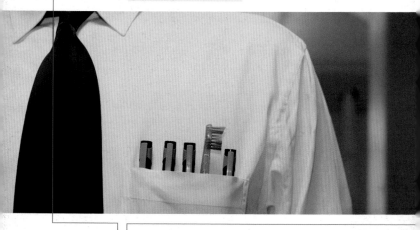

INFO TO GO

If you feel like you DON'T need to balance your relationship and work, please go to
www.divorce-lawyers-r-us.com

DON'T FIGURE OUT YOUR PRIORITIES WHILE LYING ON YOUR DEATHBED.

We've all heard the expression, "No one on their deathbed ever wished they'd spent more time at the office." Well, duh. Of course. But what about a life spent in a career that's not worth loving? Ten or 20 or 30 years spent slogging away without meaning? A study by Al Reis on retirees reported that 75% of them regretted not switching jobs at some point. How sad is that?

Loving your career doesn't require working more hours, or missing the moments of life outside of work. In fact, loving your career might mean cutting back to part-time work, or going back to school, or moving closer to family. The point is to look back from your deathbed, and feel exhilarated by your choices. Our minutes become days become weeks become months become years become the sudden realization that there's no more looking forward, only looking back.

THE ICON SAYS

"Live life as if it's a terminal illness, because if you do you will live it with joy and passion, as it ought to be lived."
—WRITER ANNA QUINDLEN

A FULL LIFE IS IMPOSSIBLE WITHOUT JOY AT WORK.

If you're buzzing about work, feeling inspired and fulfilled, you're a better friend, spouse, family member, and all else. Conversely, if you're not your best self at work, how could you be your best self anywhere?

REAL DEAL ANECDOTE

Dentists have a suicide rate that's 6.64 times higher than the working-age population. Which makes sense, considering the expression on your face when told you have to get a filling. (I'm a sugar junkie. I know that expression well.)

Source: Researcher Steven Stack

ESCAPE TOXIC.

A bad job isn't all that fun to go to in the morning. There might be politics, pressures, or boundaries in your way. Maybe it's a bad job because it keeps you from building equity in your career, or maybe it just lacks passion.

A toxic job, on the other hand, is much, much worse. In a toxic job, your opinion of yourself begins to plummet. A toxic job damages your soul. It destroys your self-confidence, it undermines your self-esteem, and it comes with very expensive therapy bills. Just as you "live up to" the high expectations of your supporters, so will you "live down to" to the low expectations of your detractors.

How can you escape, or even avoid, toxic jobs? Create enough portable equity to always have the choice of leaving from a position of power.

If you're in a bad job, take the time you need to intelligently prime yourself for the next job. If you're in a toxic job, get out.

Pronto.

94

YOU ARE A WORK IN PROGRESS.

We're all figuring it out as we go. We're all learning.
If you're not there yet, keep trying. Often the process to get
there is more valuable than actually reaching the destination.

I'm a work in progress too.

May I ask for your help? This is the first book I've ever written. How's it
going? What's working? What's not? Help me make this book, and myself,
better. I'll personally read every email (the only caveat being that as per
Truth #90, I won't always have the opportunity to respond). To contribute
your opinions (good or bad) and your ideas (good or bad), please go to
www.sally-performance-review.com. I'm ready. Bring it on.

If you are alive today, someone went to
unreasonable lengths to carry you, birth
you, watch over you. And she didn't do it
so you could grow up to be ordinary.

Refuse to carry
a membership card
to the lowest common
denominator.

〜

REMEMBER WHO YOU ARE

FIND YOUR PISTACHIO.

Not everyone likes pistachio. But for the people who like pistachio, no other ice cream will do. So if there's something about you that makes you distinct, something weird and wonderful, use it to your advantage.

ULTRA CAREERIST ADVICE

ALEX BOGUSKY ON PISTACHIOSITY

As executive creative director of Crispin Porter + Bogusky, Alex creates inimitable advertising for clients such as MINI, Virgin, and Burger King. Alex's advice for companies, and people, who want to avoid becoming vanilla:

- Nothing should be off-limits for reinvention.

- You're not right for everyone. And don't try to be. Focus on the people and companies who are about the same things you are.

- Approach every assignment as an opportunity to differentiate yourself. Every single one.

- Practice "idea obsolescence" by constantly outdoing yourself. Make your own best ideas obsolete (before someone else does it for you).

INFO TO GO

Want to boost your pistachio factor?
Go to **www.anti-vanilla.com**.

TRUST YOUR GUT. *IT'S SMARTER THAN YOU.*

Sometimes you just have a feeling about a person, a conversation, a deal. If your mind and your gut don't agree, listen carefully to your gut. It often knows something you don't.

97

DO WHAT
YOU ARE.

To reach your ultimate potential, you have to fully express yourself. We all express ourselves differently, but whether you're a firecracker or a gentle soul, your best career is an expression of yourself. What you *do* should reflect who you *are*.

This goes for any profession: a CEO, a student, an assembly line worker, or a full-time mom.

You can be truly great only when you can truly be yourself.

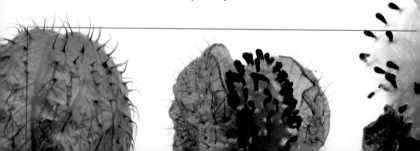

FINDING YOUR "SO THAT"

What's the true underlying purpose for your actions? I call this a "so that." You do one thing so that you can get something so that you can achieve an end result. Knowing your ultimate "so that" helps you be happier in all that you do. For instance, while people often list "money" as a goal, in fact, money isn't an end in itself. It's a "so that" for security, or respect, or contribution.

In reality, a goal is often only a superficial objective, which hides a deeper intention, which leads to an ultimate purpose. Here's a snazzy diagram:

SUPERFICIAL OBJECTIVE *[so that]* **DEEPER INTENTION** *[so that]* **ULTIMATE PURPOSE**

Here's an example. Say your goal is to earn a promotion for the prestige, pay hike, and so on. But if you think about it, you might realize the promotion is only a superficial objective. Your deeper intention is so that you'll have more flexibility over your schedule, so that you can enjoy your ultimate purpose: weekends off with family. Here's what that looks like:

PROMOTION *[so that]* **FLEXIBILITY OVER SCHEDULE** *[so that]* **MORE TIME WITH FAMILY**

If your "so that" is to enjoy more time with family, the promotion is only a means to an end. It's important to weigh that against the time investment required to earn a promotion in the first place.

98

YOU WERE BORN
UNLIKE ANY OTHER.

You arrived into this world totally and completely you.
Boy or girl, wrinkled or plump, brown eyes or blue, you
were miraculous perfection because you were nothing less
than yourself. You were *born* a careerist.

But then, somehow, it happened. You grew up.

You traded being yourself for being polite. You stopped
asking for your heart's desire, and started asking permission.

Are you ready to be nothing less than yourself once again?

What makes you you?

Who can you be that no one else is?

Once you find it, own it. Embody yourself.
Become even more you.

That's not just your career.
That's your life's work.

99,999,999 didn't make it.
You did.

THE ICON SAYS

"Figure out who you are and then do it on purpose."
—DOLLY PARTON

99

EXPRESSING YOUR TRUEST SELF IS THE ULTIMATE COMPETITIVE ADVANTAGE.

Traditional corporate culture induces mind-numbing homogeny. Success requires fitting in. The game is to get the "right" suit, the "right" handshake, the "right" letterhead. Hundreds of books tell you how to be right.

But "right" is standard. Boring.
And frankly, beneath you.

Being a careerist means being the biggest,
best version of yourself.

Never dumb yourself down,
or think less interesting thoughts.

Never compromise your innate advantages.

Never confuse a cubicle with a pigeonhole.

INFO
TO GO

What is your truest self? Find it at
www.ultimate-competitive-advantage.com.

100

MAKE YOUR MEMOIRS WORTH READING.

A career that makes you fulfilled and proud isn't the most important piece of your life. Not at all. But it is a piece. An essential piece. To kill time in an uninspiring job, then another, and another, and then one day look back on a lifetime of meaningless effort...how tragic.

Years from now, when we're old and retired and reflecting upon our lives, may no part remain unlived, no opportunity squandered, no talent wasted, no aspiration unfulfilled.

A possibility lives within you.

A possibility of a career so
extraordinary that it deserves
your time, your talents,
your heart.

What is your possibility?

What extraordinary
potential awaits?

Find it. Bring it forth.
Make it your life.

Because when you do, you'll have
your career worth loving.

A.

1B4

d

ODUCTS
ON,
.

m or by
retrieval
reviewer

t:

N-12679
CIP

CAREERING OXYMORONS

1. SAFE IS RISKY

2. PROBLEMS ARE OPPORTUNITY

3. LONG-TERM SOLUTIONS ARE TEMPORARY

4. SAY NO TO "YES MEN"

5. GOOD RELATIONSHIPS ARE WORTH FIGHTING FOR

6. BUILDING UP GROWTH REQUIRES BREAKING DOWN BARRIERS

7. PERFECTION IS MESSY

8. GROW SMALLER

9. JARGON SAYS NOTHING

10. DIFFICULTY IS POSSIBILITY

A BRIEF HISTORY OF CAREERISTS

Careering isn't a newfangled approach. Since the dawn of time, careerists have advanced their careers, and mankind, by refusing the status quo.

The first guy to make fire
#9: FORGET WHAT YOUR BUSINESS CARD SAYS. YOU'RE AN ENTREPRENEUR.

RADICAL
CAREERING
WEBSITE

*Ready to fire up your shiny new
radical careering skills?*

Let's go.

Online you'll find all kinds of
crazycool tools, insight, and inspiration
to kick your career into high gear.

www.RADICALCAREERING.com

PHOTO CREDITS

The photography in this book couldn't have been possible without the help of my brilliant image partner, Getty Images. All my thanks to Peggy Willett and her team, and to the Getty Images photographers and art directors whose extraordinary talents produced the following images, in order of appearance:

BU003629
Don Farrall

BU003630
Don Farrall

200010291-001
David Madison

200173668-001
Garry Hunter

200011485-001
David Sacks

200154369-001
Henrik Weis

comks6079
Comstock Images

DES_056
Photodisc Collection

200156429-001
Andrew Michael

304615-001
S Purdy Matthews

*csaimages.com

WL004029
Arthur S Aubry

YOF_095
Photodisc Collection

70000612
Archive Holdings Inc

200151352-001
Microzoa

200164326-001
Thomas J Peterson

dv1576093
Hans-Peter Merten

ma0309-001
Ernst Haas

DES_006
Photodisc Collection

AG001698
Siede Preis

200130500-001
Laurence Dutton

bd5955-001
Howard Kingsnorth

200156313-001
Andrew Michael

NA006506
Don Tremain

200069722-001
John Slater

3170577
John Kobal Foundation

200144118-001
Steve Taylor

AA014130
David Toase

NA004371
PhotoLink

bd2257-001
Sean Ellis

bd4231-001
Tim Flach

imsis252-007
Image Source

ec5942-001
GK Hart/Vicky Hart

comks5996
Comstock Images

200139671-001
Paul Viant

la4985-001
Davies & Starr

comks6073
Comstock Images

818887-003
Dietrich Rose

200023653-001
Andy Sacks

478796
Michel Tcherevkoff

200025092-001
Timothy Archibald

skd190157sdc
Stockdisc

bc8437-001
Brendan Beirne

10106818
Pete Turner

SPE_064
Photodisc Collection

200112447-001
Jack Ambrose

la7574-001
Davies & Starr

bd6208-001
Robert Daly

889325-001
Mark Harris

200026374-001
Gary S & Vivian Chapman

ga10143
David Ponton

la9682-001
Alex Freund

bf1437-001
Jim Naughten

200178265-003
Alex & Laila

fpx20960
John Burwell

ec6406-001
Bill Steele

976340-004
Doug Struthers

891789-001
Catherine Ledner

*Number 17

Special Thanks to
Bob Stevens for his
author photo.
www.bobstevens.com

*courtesy of as noted

For more images to inspire your own radical ideas,
please visit **www.gettyimages.com**.

ACKNOWLEDGEMENTS

The two-year process of developing Radical Careering required some hardcore radical careering. It forced me to enact every single one of the Radical Truths at least once, if not twice.

First and always, thank you to my beloved husband. You make my job, my career, and my life possible. And to our two sweetiepies, for being so insanely adorable. I love you with all my heart.

I also had the honor of working with extraordinarily talented people. A few in particular to whom I give my warmest thanks:

To Sabrina Ross Lee, my advisor and muse, for her invaluable contribution.

To my agent, Jeff Herman; my publisher, Bill Shinker; my editor, Lauren Marino; and the whole team at Penguin who joined in the "radical publishing." Thank you for staying true to the vision.

To my executive producer, the incomparable Liz Walker.

To Bryan Chiao, for emailing ideas at 5 a.m.

To Number 17 for pulling fabulous design rabbits out of hats.

Finally, to my dearest family. To Mutti and Big D, for embodying timeless careerist qualities: daily overachieving, unconditional support, and relentless optimism. And to Andy and Nancy, for being my role models since the days of the Champion Milk Drinking Contests.